FOREIGN LOANS
AND ECONOMIC
PERFORMANCE

FOREIGN LOANS AND ECONOMIC PERFORMANCE

The Experience
of the
Less Developed Countries

by

Ehsan Nikbakht

PRAEGER

PRAEGER SPECIAL STUDIES • PRAEGER SCIENTIFIC

New York • Philadelphia • Eastbourne, UK
Toronto • Hong Kong • Tokyo • Sydney

Library of Congress Cataloging in Publication Data

Nikbakht, Ehsan.
  Foreign loans and economic performance.

  Bibliography: p.
  Includes index.
  1. Loans, Foreign—Developing countries. 2. Debt,
External—Developing countries. 3. Developing countries—
Economic policy. I. Title.
HG3891.5.N55   1984   336.3′435′091724   84-8296
ISBN 0-03-071436-2 (alk. paper)

Published in 1984 by Praeger Publishers
CBS Educational and Professional Publishers
a Division of CBS, Inc.
521 Fifth Avenue, New York, New York 10175, U.S.A.

© 1984 by Praeger Publishers

456789 052 987654321
Printed in the United States of America
on acid-free paper

For my daughter,
Auzin

Preface

The world today faces a major policy question: How to explain and correct the debt problem of the less developed countries (LDCs)? The significance of the problem is reflected in widely publicized news that by 1983 more than 25 non-oil-exporting LDCs rescheduled their outstanding loans, and a majority of those countries were denied additional private funds. The economies of the LDCs are inextricably interrelated with the economies of the developed countries, both from the supply side and the demand side. The LDCs are profitable markets in which the developed countries sell their consumer and capital goods and various types of services. In exchange, the developed countries demand raw material, semifinished goods, some finished goods, and the so-called petrodollars from the LDCs. Because of this continuous reciprocity, the accumulated debts and the possibility of economic stagnation in the LDCs should be perceived as worldwide financial and economic issues. The occurrence of widespread insolvency in the LDCs will further compound the existing financial problems of advanced economies. Potential risk is mutually shared both by the developed and the developing countries. Thus indifference to the issue of foreign debts in general, and the impact of debts on the economies of the LDCs in particular, is neither morally nor economically justified.

Scholars and many practitioners in the fields of finance and economics now agree that the ultimate objective of financing—whether debt or equity—is to maximize wealth. This paradigm should hold true whether it applies to financing a microentity, like a company, or a macroentity, like a country. Drawing on such a premise, this book examines whether debt financing in the form of foreign loans has led to more wealth for the LDCs. In order to make this inquiry, a host of measurable macroeconomic indicators were selected as indices of wealth. Chapter 1 explains in detail the methodology of the research. In Chapter 2 the trends of the inflow of debts to the LDCs are analyzed. Chapter 3 presents the results of the empirical analysis. The cases of Korea versus Peru are discussed in Chapter 4 to determine if the motivation (purpose and uses) for borrowing can explain the results of the statistical analysis. Finally, the research and the main conclusions are summarized in Chapter 5.

The findings of this research should be helpful and informative to policymakers, both in borrowing and lending countries. A main conclusion is that abundant external capital does not guarantee economic prosperity for developing countries. Learning that there has been no systematic relationship between foreign loans and economic performance alerts policymakers to the consequences of the decisions they made in the past. Understanding the reasons for the absence of a logical relationship between financing and development of the LDCs provides an instructive feedback that lets decision makers focus on variables and prerequisites that may have been missing or proved inadequate in economic planning. It is this contribution that the author hopes will make this book worth reading and understanding.

Acknowledgments

This study is an extended and updated version of my doctoral thesis. I am thankful to a number of people and institutions for the completion and revision of the project. In particular, I am indebted to Drs. Rodney Eldridge, Yoon Park, William Handorf, Fariborz Ghadar, Jack Zwick, Phillip Grub and Theodore Barnhill of the George Washington University. I am thankful to the staff of the External Debt Division of the World Bank, and the International Monetary Fund in Washington, D.C. for generously responding to my request for data and interviews. I thank Mr. Ismaeil Ibrahimi of the External Debt Division, and Mr. Mohammed Khishtan for their assistance in collecting data and documents. Ms. Patricia Ropp deserves thanks for her help in using statistical computer models. My gratitude to my colleagues at the Business School of Hofstra University for their comments and support. I am emotionally indebted to my wife, Parvin, for her care and patience while I was writing and extending this project.

Of course, none of the above individuals and institutions is responsible for the analysis and conclusions I have presented in this book; that burden is the author's alone.

Contents

List of Tables and Figures

LIST OF FIGURES

FOREIGN LOANS AND ECONOMIC PERFORMANCE

1

Hypothesis
and Methodology

This book is about the foreign loans of the less developed countries (LDCs). Its purpose is to present an empirical study in a comparative context regarding the level of external borrowing and economic growth of the borrowing LDCs over a period of time. The relationship between the level of external debt and economic growth is of major concern to both the lending institutions and the borrowing countries. It is unknown whether an LDC with a high level of debt inflow, compared to an LDC with a low level of debt inflow, has been associated with more favorable growth indicators over the long run. Therefore a systematic attempt to answer this important question will be a contribution to the field of external finance and development of borrowing LDCs.

Measuring the magnitude of the debt-capital inflow to LDCs, through any source and methodology, leaves the impression that LDCs have continuously increased their borrowing from public and private international financial institutions in the last ten years. (See the sources and the trends of borrowing in Chapter 2.) The impression about the volume of debt does not change whether the data are collected from the World Bank's published information on the debt of 99 member countries, the Bank for International Settlement, or the Organization for Economic Cooperation and Development, which periodically publishes the debt

1

outflow of 17 members of its Development Assistance Committee to LDCs.

Figures released by the World Bank estimate that the medium- and long-term disbursed debt outstanding of LDCs increased from $135 billion in 1974 to $298 billion in 1978 and further grew to $462 billion by the end of 1981. The estimated figure of disbursed debt outstanding of the LDCs was $529 billion in 1982.[1] Between 1973 and 1977, when the world was challenging recession and going through various adjustments, the developing countries increased their borrowing by 126 percent, equal to an annual growth of 31 percent. Adjusted for short-term financial obligations of $50 to $60 billion and outstanding International Monetary Fund credits of around $8 billion at the end of 1977, the total external debt liabilities of these countries had an average annual growth of more than 40 percent.[2]

It should be pointed out that the inflow of external debt has not been of the same magnitude or pace for all LDCs. The level of external borrowing has been different from one country to another in the last 15 years. Even in the mid-1970s, when many aggressive lenders were marketing their loans in both creditworthy and less creditworthy countries, the responses from LDCs were not the same. Some eagerly borrowed in the market while a great number stayed out, even though the terms offered were relatively favorable. As P. A. Wellons put it, some were "eager," some were "ambivalent," and some remained "reluctant." No regional or income pattern could be inferred from such classification as both lower and higher income countries of different regions were in those response groups.[3] In the light of this dichotomy of high-borrowing versus low-borrowing LDCs, this book will proceed with an inquiry as to the relationship between the level of external borrowing and economic performance.

The normative relationship between the level of borrowing (capital) and economic performance is theoretically or conceptually justified in the existing literature. The Harrod-Domar theory of capital formation related the growth of an economy to its savings-income ratio and marginal capital output ratio.[4] The implication is that a country with no sufficient domestic savings has to make up the capital shortage through the inflow of new funds before it reaches target growth. Avramovic et al. also suggest that the growth capacity of the borrowing LDCs in the early stage of development is limited by domestic resources to finance the target growth. Therefore external borrowing as a source of capital inflow will lead the borrowing countries into a successful "growth-cum-debt" cycle.[5]

In most studies of external finance and development, capital either in the form of debt or equity has maintained a major position. Various authors have consistently stressed the role of capital, whether in historical studies of industrial revolution, in analytical models to explain the growth of an economy, or in recommended policies for development.[6] The popular theory of the "two gap" exemplifies such a dominant role of capital in the literature.[7]

According to this theory, capital inflow accelerates development in two ways. On the one hand, it fills the gap between internal sources of financing (savings) and internal funds required for development (investment). On the other, capital inflow generates sufficient foreign exchange to fill the gap between the import expenditure and export revenue. Therefore growth of a borrowing LDC is restricted by these internal and external gaps. In an attempt to decrease these gaps, the developing economies have to participate in various international capital markets to import sufficient capital either in the form of aid, borrowing, or direct investment. Early growth models, such as the Alter aid-requirement model, are also based on the same premise.[8]

A very poor country does not have and cannot generate sufficient funds to finance the target growth. Its savings portion of income is very low at the outset of development. Hence external capital is the only source to balance the investment expenditures and total savings. In the process of importing capital the rate of income gradually improves and finally equals the rate of investment plus a surplus to offset the cost of imported capital, that is, interest and dividends. It is such a theoretically meaningful cause-effect sequence that may justify the policies of LDCs to tap various markets for imported capital. The unknown question is whether such a theoretical relationship has actually held true in the case of borrowing LDCs. To answer this question, this book will focus on research for a selected group of borrowing LDCs for which data are complete and available from 1963 to 1979.

A word of clarification is in order. Economic growth and development is a value concept that has different definitions and may serve different purposes for different people. Some may view growth and development as the process of social equity and justice, level of leisure and quality of life, and the like. Others view growth and development in terms of objective and measurable criteria of economic performance. Throughout this book the author will deal with the latter concept, namely, a host of measurable indices of economic performance (macroeconomic indicators).

True, gathering data for the debt and economic indicators of the borrowing LDCs, making analyses, and proving
or rejecting a hypothesis is not an easy and straightforward
task. Diversity of the sources of the data is still a research problem. Different sources, depending on their
computation methodology, usually report different values for
the same variable in the same year. Reporting one variable
in a local currency and the other in U.S. dollars or SDRs
(special drawing rights) may easily mislead the researcher
in a comparative cross-country analysis. A conversion
rate, whether it is an arithmetic average or a geometric
average of twelve months, four quarters, or simply the
ending period exchange rate may give different results in
the comparison of two economies. However, after verification and elimination of doubtful data, and using consistent
sources and consistent computational procedures, such
potential errors can be reduced.

Furthermore, researchers should be encouraged by the
fact that the quality of most data of the developing countries has been improved for the more recent years. The
World Bank Debt Reporting System, which started in the
early 1950s, has been periodically revised and significantly
upgraded in the 1970s. *World Debt Tables* report the
external public as well as publicly guaranteed private debt
of 99 countries. The detailed data are regularly provided
by member countries to the World Bank through standard-
ized forms with necessary instructions. The data are then
prepared in various standard tables for each country by
the staff of the External Debt Division of the Economic
Analysis and Projections Department of the Bank.

In addition to statistical analysis of the economic data of
the borrowing LDCs, the research also includes two cases,
Korea and Peru. The criteria for the selection of these two
countries are explained in the methodology section. These
two cases reflect additional facts that are almost impossible
to construe merely out of statistical tests and derived
ratios.

FORMULATION OF A HYPOTHESIS

A comparative study of growth indicators for a group of
borrowing countries could be done according to source of
external financing (private versus public), level of total
capital inflow, level of borrowing versus level of direct
investment, level of direct investment only, and/or level of
external borrowing only. The purpose of this research is
to make a comparative study of growth indicators only

according to the level of external borrowing of LDCs. Therefore the research hypothesis is formulated as follows: A higher level of external debt capital inflow is associated with relatively more favorable values for economic growth indicators of a developing country over the long run, that is, a borrowing LDC with a higher level of external debt inflow, compared to an LDC with a lower level of debt inflow, maintains more favorable economic growth indicators in the same period of external borrowing.

It is important to note that the growth indicators of two borrowing countries with different levels of borrowing could be compared if they have had rather similar equity capital inflow. The fulfillment of this important condition is required to minimize the effect of the equity capital inflow on the values of growth indicators.

Considering this condition, the study will attempt to answer one major question and one supplementary question: Major question: Comparing two countries with similar equity capital inflow but different levels of external borrowing, did the country with a higher level of external borrowing maintain more favorable growth indicators during a specified period of borrowing? Supplementary question: What has been the motivation (purpose and uses) of the external borrowing? Did the motivation influence the values of growth indicators (a case study approach)?

It is mainly the answer to the "major question" that tends to prove, reject, or make inconclusive the stated hypothesis.

METHODOLOGY OF THE RESEARCH

The following macroeconomic indicators, referred to here as "economic growth indicators," have been selected as indices of economic growth based on their theoretical foundation, availability of data, and measurability of their values:

Incremental capital output ratio (ICOR)
Marginal savings ratio
Average savings ratio
Growth rate of export
Growth rate of gross domestic product (GDP)
Ratio of export to GDP
External gap (export-import)
Internal gap (savings-investment)
Net resource transfer on account of debt capital

(See the appendix for the theoretical reasoning for the use of these various economic indicators in this research.)

The basic approach to answer the major question is ranking and pairing the sample countries, running paired *t*-tests and multiple regressions for the annual values of the selected economic indicators. This statistical work is supplemented by separate case studies of Korea and Peru to answer the supplementary question.

The primary sample includes 20 borrowing LDCs, some of which are major borrowers according to World Bank statistics. In order to improve the homogeneity of the borrowing countries in the sample, the author has excluded OPEC members, centrally planned economies, lower-income-group countries (less than $550 per capita income), and higher-income-group countries (more than $2,500 per capita income). Availability of the data for the period under study has been another reason to prefer one country over another in constructing the primary sample. However, the sample includes both the major and ordinary borrowing LDCs (see Table 1-1).

TABLE 1-1. A Sample of 20 Borrowing LDCs

1.	Argentina	11.	Jordan
2.	Brazil	12.	Korea
3.	Chile	13.	Malaysia
4.	Columbia	14.	Mexico
5.	Costa Rica	15.	Panama
6.	Cyprus	16.	Paraguay
7.	Dominican Republic	17.	Peru
8.	Ecuador	18.	Portugal
9.	Guatemala	19.	Tunisia
10.	Jamaica	20.	Turkey

Notes: The OPEC countries and the centrally planned economies were excluded, as were LDCs with less than $550 per capita income (lower income) and LDCs with more than $2,500 per capita income higher income). The World Bank list of countries by income group as reported in Borrowing in International Capital Markets (EC-181/794) is the base of this country grouping. Countries in the sample that represent both the principal and ordinary borrowers were selected on the basis of availability of data.

The study goes through 13 steps in sequence. The primary purpose of steps 1 to 9 is to derive from the sample at least five pairs of borrowing countries with the following characteristics: The countries in each pair, on the average, have similar monetary values of direct investment, adjusted for size, in the period under study. Also, the countries in each pair, on the average, have different values of debt inflow, adjusted for size, in the period under study.

The importance of this pairing process lies in the fact that it helps neutralize or minimize the effect of equity capital, as a major source of capital inflow, on growth indicators. The following steps will be taken in sequence:

1. Values for equity capital inflow are gathered for individual countries in the sample from 1963 to 1977. The years 1978 and 1979 are dropped for a lead-and-lag purpose. The values of equity are the monetary values of "direct investment," as reported in millions of SDR in Table 2, Section B, of *Balance of Payments Yearbook.**

2. The above data are adjusted for size (direct investment/GDP of the same year). The exchange rate between SDR and the local currency from line "aa" of the Exchange Rates section in *International Financial Statistics* is used to convert annual GDP figures into SDR.

3. The average annual monetary values of direct investment, adjusted for size, of individual countries in the sample are calculated for the period under study.

4. The countries are rank-ordered according to the above values of direct investment, adjusted for size.

5. The data for annual debt inflow are gathered for the same individual countries. These data are the figures for "total all lenders—disbursement," as reported in U.S. dollars in various issues of *World Debt Tables*. These debts include public and public-guaranteed medium- and long-term debt plus private medium- and long-term debt (publicly guaranteed) as collected by the World Bank from member countries.§

6. The above figures are adjusted for size ("total all lenders—outstanding disbursed only" divided by GDP of the same year). The annual arithmetic means of the U.S. dollar rates for local currencies from line "rf" of the Exchange Rates section of *International Financial Statistics* is used to convert GDP figures into U.S. dollars.

7. The average values of debt inflow, adjusted for size, of individual countries are calculated for the period under study.

---

*See step 10 for a complete listing of all sources.

§These debts exclude transactions with the International Monetary Fund, nonpublicly guaranteed private debts, short-term debts, and debts denominated in home currencies. For details, see *World Debt Tables* (various issues).

8.   The borrowing countries are rank-ordered according to the above values of debt inflow adjusted for size.

9.   After comparing the countries ranked in step 4 (according to the level of direct investment) and in step 8 (according to the level of debt inflow), the pairs of borrowing LDCs that best meet the pairing criteria are selected.   Restating the criteria briefly, the countries in each pair have the most similar levels of direct investment and the most different debt inflow in the sample.   The similarity in the levels of direct investment and the differences in the levels of debt inflow are verified through paired t-tests as well.

10.   For the countries paired in step 9, values of the macroeconomic indicators are collected from 1965 to 1979. Note that there is a two-year lag between the year of external borrowing and the year when economic indicators are affected.   Therefore the years 1963 and 1964 are ignored in computing the values of those indicators.   The annual values for each growth indicator are derived based on the raw data collected mainly from the following sources:

International Financial Statistics
(International Monetary Fund)

International Financial Statistics Yearbook
(International Monetary Fund)

Balance of Payments Yearbook
(International Monetary Fund)

World Debt Tables
(World Bank)

Yearbook of National Accounts Statistics
(United Nations)

The specific source of each variable, the way the values are computed, and the procedure for conversion of different currencies are presented in Table 1–2.

11.   Using the *Statistical Package for the Social Sciences,* paired t-tests are run to determine if the average values of the annual differences of individual growth indicators are significantly different between the countries in each pair.[9] It should be noted that in this test, the main emphasis is on the annual differences, *not* the overall means of individual growth indicators.   For illustration, the growth indicator xg—the growth in export of the paired countries A versus B—is put into the following format:

Year	Country A	Country B	Annual Difference
1965	$xg65$	$xg65$	$(xg65)A-(xg65)B$
1966	$xg66$	$xg66$	$(xg66)A-(xg66)B$
1967	$xg67$	$xg67$	$(xg67)A-(xg67)B$
.	.	.	.
.	.	.	.
.	.	.	.
1979	$xg79$	$xg79$	$(xg79)A-(xg79)B$

Having seven pairs of countries and nine growth indicators in the final study, the author runs 63 (7 × 9) paired t-tests accordingly. The results are put into a matrix table showing the indicators whose values are significantly different or insignificantly different for the countries in each pair. The format may be illustrated as follows:

Indicators

Paired Countries	$x1$	$x2$	$x3$	...	$x9$
A vs. B	diff.	diff.	diff.	...	diff.
C vs. D	not diff.	not diff.	not diff.	...	not diff.
E vs. F	not diff.	not diff.	not diff.	...	....
G vs. H	....	....	....	...	....
I vs. J	....	....	....	...	....

diff. = significantly different; not diff. = insignificantly different.

In the case of a possible dominant pattern of "significantly different" values, the result tends to accept the hypothesis. In the absence of a very visible dominant pattern in the table, the next contingency is a test for the "dichotomous data." This test generally classifies the observed data into one of two classes based on the absence or presence of a certain characteristic. One of the two dichotomies is "insignificantly different" and the other is "significantly different" values. The former category is assigned "0" and the other "1." The test will basically attempt to determine if there is any difference between the percentage of 0's and the percentage of 1's in the table.[10]

12. In further attempts to determine if a higher level of external borrowing has been associated with more favorable values for growth indicators, the author also runs multiple regression tests for all seven high-borrowing countries in

TABLE 1-2. Calculation Procedure for Values of Economic Indicators

1. Incremental capital output ratio (ICOR) is calculated as the ratio of the "gross capital formation" to the annual change in the "gross domestic products." Considering a two-year lag in computation, this formula is used consistently for all countries:

ICOR = Capital formation/GDP - GDP
($\underline{t}$)   ($\underline{t}$-2)   ($\underline{t}$)   ($\underline{t}$-1)

Values for capital formation and GDP were gathered from the National Accounts section of International Financial Statistics Yearbook, lines 93 and 99b, respectively.

2. Marginal savings ratio is determined by the ratio of the annual change in "time and savings deposits" to the annual change in the "gross domestic products." The data for "time and savings deposits" and the "gross domestic products" were gathered from lines 25 and 99b, respectively, of International Financial Statistics.

3. Average savings ratio is derived by the ratio of the annual "time and savings deposit" to the "gross domestic products." The sources are the same as in number 2.

4. Growth rate of export is calculated by the annual percentage increase or decrease in "Merchandise: Export F.O.B.," as reported in Table 1, Section A, of Balance of Payments Yearbook. The values are reported in SDR.

5. GDP growth is the annual percentage increase or decrease of the "gross domestic product" from the source in number 1. GDP figures are deflated based on the local Consumer Price Index reported in line 64, Price Section, of International Financial Statistics for individual countries.

6. The ratio of export to GDP is the ratio of "Merchandise: Export F.O.B." reported in SDR to the "gross domestic product" reported in the local currency. The exchange rate between SDR and the local currency from line aa of the Exchange Rates Section of International Financial Statistics has been used for conversion of the currencies.

7. External gap (export-import), adjusted for size, is the ratio of the trade balance to the "gross domestic product." The former is collected from Table 1.A of Balance of Payments Yearbook, reported in SDR, and the latter from the source in number 1. The procedure for conversion of the currencies is the same as number 6.

8. Internal gap (savings-investment), adjusted for size, is the difference between the values of "time and savings deposits" and "gross capital formation" divided by "gross domestic products." The sources are the same in numbers 1 and 2.

9. Net resource transfer on account of debt capital is determined by subtracting the values of the "principal payment" and the "interest payment" from the "disbursement," as reported in the External Debt section by type of creditor in World Debt Tables.

Note: For the sake of consistency in data, the author has tried to derive as many ratios as possible from the same source of data.

the paired sample. To reduce multicollinearity (interdependence) of the variables, only four macroeconomic indicators from the nine indicators are incorporated in the test. The incremental capital output ratio (ICOR), the marginal savings ratio, the growth rate of export, and the growth rate of GDP have been selected on the ground that they are relatively independent, each reflecting a separate concept about the performance of the economy. A two-year lag is considered in running the tests for the period under study. (See the details and results of the tests in Chapter 3.)

13. The purpose of the previous steps was to answer the major research question. The methodology was mainly quantitative. In an attempt to answer the supplementary question, two borrowing LDCs from the sample are studied in qualitative terms as well. The purpose is to see if the motivation (purpose and uses) of borrowing has influenced the values of growth indicators in the period under study.

Korea and Peru were selected for study for the following reasons: (1) The results in Chapter 3 reveal that Korea, as a major borrower in the sample, is the only country whose level of borrowing has been consistently associated with favorable values of growth indicators; (2) unlike Korea, Peru, which is also a major borrower in the sample, maintained consistently unfavorable values of growth indicators in the period under study; (3) the size of the economy of Peru expressed in terms of GDP, relative to those of other high-borrowing countries in the sample, is the largest and therefore closest to that of Korea; and (4) the data for Korea and Peru are available for the purpose of the case study.

LIMITATIONS AND CAVEATS

The scope of this study is limited to the test of a normative hypothesis about the relationship between the level of external borrowing and the values of economic performance. Thus the study does not include various other factors, such as management of economy, social and economic planning, sociopolitical institutions, ideology, culture, and history, that might affect the values of economic performance in the long run. The scope of the study is also limited by the number of borrowing LDCs in the sample. Excluding the low-income and high-income LDCs, the sample includes 20 middle-income non-OPEC LDCs that have been carefully selected to represent both the major and ordinary borrowing countries.

The data base for external loans is the World Bank Debtor Reporting System, which publishes the debt of public debtors and publicly guaranteed private debtors in the annual *World Debt Tables*. Thus the debt of nonguaranteed private debtors is excluded from these data. This exclusion should not be a major limitation in this study, however, because the phenomenon of aggressive private borrowing in general, and of nonguaranteed private borrowing in particular, is relatively low. Besides, the data for nonguaranteed private debt are not yet fully developed. The recently published data for such debt by the World Bank Debtor Reporting System and the Organization for Economic Cooperation and Development Creditor Reporting System are very partial.

CONCLUSION

Borrowing by LDCs has dramatically increased in the 1970s and 1980s. The existing body of empirical research in the area of finance and growth does not show whether a higher level of foreign loans has led to a higher level of economic performance. This book, through the collection and challenge of the data from various sources, statistical analysis, and case study, will focus on such an important question.

The major caveat of this study is the fact that the final conclusion(s) should not categorically be generalized to the total universe of LDCs from which 20 have been selected. Yet these countries have been selected based on a set of criteria to maximize the generality of the findings. With those qualifications in mind, the author proceeds with the analysis and conclusions in the following chapters.

NOTES

1. *World Debt Tables* (Washington, D.C.: World Bank 1983), p. xiii.

2. Jeffrey A. Katz, *Capital Flows and Developing Country Debt*, Working Paper no. 352 (Washington, D.C.: World Bank, August 1979), p. 3.

3. P. A. Wellons, *Borrowing by Developing Countries on the Euro-Currency Market* (Paris: OECD 1977), p. 48.

4. Benjamin Higgins, *Economic Development Problems, Principles and Policies* (New York: Norton 1968), p. 118.

5. D. Avramovic et al., *Economic Growth and External Debt* (Baltimore: Johns Hopkins University Press 1964), pp. 53–55.

6. A. K. Cairncross, "The Place of Capital in Economic Progress," in *Leading Issues in Economic Development,* ed,

Gerald M. Meier (New York: Oxford University Press, 1976), p. 261.

7. H. B. Chenery, and A. M. Strout, "Foreign Assistance and Economic Development," *American Economic Review* 56 (September 1966): 680–90.

8. Gerald M. Alter, "The Servicing of Foreign Capital Inflows by Underdeveloped Countries," in *Economic Development of Latin America,* ed. Howard S. Ellis (New York: St. Martin's Press 1963).

9. See Norman H. Nie et al., *The SPSS Batch System for the DEC PDPII* (New York: McGraw-Hill 1980), pp. 101–04.

10. B. J. Winer, *Statistical Principles of Experimental Design,* 2nd edit. (New York: McGraw-Hill 1971), pp. 44–50.

2

A Review of
the Aggregated Debt Inflow
to LDCs

This chapter examines the trends and sources of the debt inflow to LDCs. The source of the data is basically the Debt Reporting System of the World Bank, which is based on regular reports from the Bank's member countries. The reported data of the member countries are organized by the staff of the External Debt Division of the Economic Analysis and Projections Department of the Bank and are published in the annual *World Debt Tables*. Another source of the data is the annual reports of the Bank for International Settlements. The latter data are from the Creditor Reporting System of the Organization for Economic Cooperation and Development. After categorization and necessary computations, the data are presented in several tables for discussion purposes.

CLASSIFICATION OF LOANS TO LDCs

There are several ways in which external loans of LDCs can be categorized. One way is according to their source, that is, the organizations that provide loans. An alternative classification is based on the type of loan—official versus private or concessional versus nonconcessional. Yet, in every classification the problem of overlap exists. With this limitation in mind, a diagram to classify the major LDC loans is offered in Figure 2–1; it will be used as the framework of the forthcoming discussion.

Figure 2-1. External Loans of LDCs

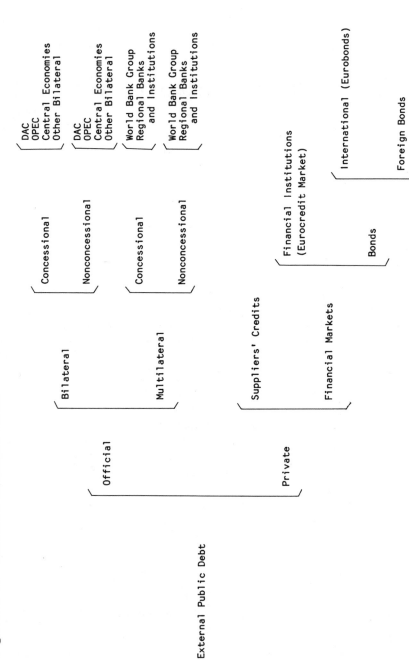

External Public Debt

Official
- Bilateral
  - Concessional
    - DAC
    - OPEC
    - Central Economies
    - Other Bilateral
  - Nonconcessional
    - DAC
    - OPEC
    - Central Economies
    - Other Bilateral
- Multilateral
  - Concessional
    - World Bank Group
    - Regional Banks
    - and Institutions
  - Nonconcessional
    - World Bank Group
    - Regional Banks
    - and Institutions

Private
- Suppliers' Credits
- Financial Markets
  - Financial Institutions (Eurocredit Market)
  - Bonds
    - International (Eurobonds)
    - Foreign Bonds

Using the definitions of the Debt Reporting System of the World Bank, the external public debt in Figure 2-1 covers all types of debt "owed to non-residents, and repayable in foreign currency, goods or services that ha[ve] an original or extended maturity of one year."[1] The external public debt is classified into two broad categories: official and private. An official debt is the obligation of a public borrower, including the national government, a political subdivision, and autonomous public bodies.[2] An official debt may be granted in either bilateral or multilateral arrangements. Bilateral flows are the resources that are transferred from one country to another; multilateral flows are those resources that come from international or regional institutions. According to the classification in Figure 2-1, both bilateral and multilateral flows may be either concessional or nonconcessional. Because the concept of concessionality is a complicated one, some clarification about the dichotomy of concessional versus nonconcessional is in order.

The concessionality of a loan depends on the value of its "grant equivalent." Suppose the World Bank lends $1 million to a country X with an interest rate of 3 percent for a maturity of twenty years, to be repaid in equal installments starting after a grace period of five years on the principal. In this arrangement, country X has to pay $30,000 interest for the first five years and annual installments of $67,217.71 for the next twenty years. If the market rate, which is a critical variable, equals 6 percent, the present value of the scheduled repayments is $702,487. This leads to an inflow (benefit) of $1 million to country X and an outflow (cost) of $702,487. The net benefit is simply the difference between the two values ($1,000,000 - $702,487 = $297,513), or, by definition, a "grant equivalent" of 29.7 percent.[3] Such a loan, assuming all the assumptions are valid, represents a concessional loan. The World Bank has consistently used a 10 percent rate to discount future payments in its classification of concessional and nonconcessional loans. Thus this classification is subject to any limitations of the 10% arbitrary discount rate.

As stated, bilateral and multilateral loans can be either concessional or nonconcessional. The major providers of bilateral loans are the members of the Development Assistance Committee (DAC) of the Organization for Economic Cooperation and Development (OECD): Austria, Belgium, Canada, Denmark, England, France, Germany, Italy, Japan, the Netherlands, New Zealand, Norway, Sweden, Switzerland, and the United States. They periodically set a finance target for their Official Development Assistance

(ODA) to LDCs. Members of DAC are not the only official bilateral creditors of LDCs. Members of OPEC, as well as the centrally planned economies, are also among the bilateral lenders in both concessional and nonconcessional terms (see Figure 2–1).

With respect to multilateral loans, the category includes the World Bank group, consisting of the International Bank for Reconstruction and Development (IBRD), the International Finance Corporation (IFC), and the International Development Assistance (IDA); and regional banks and institutions, such as the Inter-American Development Bank (IBD), the African Development Bank (AFDB), the Asian Development Bank (ADB), the Central American Bank for Economic Integration (CABEI), and the European Investment Bank (EIB).

Private debt inflows to LDCs have been divided into suppliers' credits and financial markets. Suppliers' credits are basically medium-term credits extended by manufacturers, exporters, and other suppliers to the government agencies or private institutions of the LDCs that purchase goods and services in overseas markets. Financial markets are private banks and other financial institutions that offer medium-term and long-term loans to governments, government agencies, and private institutions of LDCs. Financial markets can be further subclassified into financial institutions (mainly the Eurocredit market) and the bond market (mainly the Eurobond market). A major portion of the loans in financial institutions is in the form of Eurocredits whose Eurodollar portion has been dominant.[4] The Eurocredit market, as one of the Eurofinancial markets, provides medium- and long-term loans to borrowers through syndicated banks. In fact, a comprehensive term for this market is "syndicated medium-term Eurocurrency rollover credit."[5]

The last category of loans to LDCs is the bond market, which consists of international bonds (Eurobonds) and foreign bonds. International bonds (or Eurobonds) are denominated in a currency other than that of the borrower and underwritten and offered simultaneously in different national markets. Foreign bonds are usually underwritten and offered by a group of bankers in a specific country and denominated in that country's currency.

Using the classification in Figure 2–1, the trend for each category of loans will be reviewed in the next section.

THE TREND OF EXTERNAL LOANS OF LDCs

Most of the discussions in the literature about the aggregated debt of LDCs are made in terms of the stock of debt rather than the annual inflow of debt. The stock of debt, reflected in the value of "debt outstanding and disbursed" or "debt outstanding including undisbursed," is often misleading because these accumulated values do not reflect the annual inflow of debt to LDCs. A trend analysis based on the stock of debt merely suggests the magnitude of leverage (debt financing) or total obligations of the borrower at the end of the year. In order to identify in what specific years borrowers shifted from one source to another or became more aggressive in borrowing, the data for the annual disbursed loans are more relevant. Thus, in this section, the data for the annual disbursed debt will be examined. However, in the absence of the values of annual disbursed debt for certain categories of loans, their outstanding values (stock of debt) will be reviewed.

Table 2-1 indicates that the total official and private debt (disbursed) to LDCs has dramatically increased from $14.3 billion in 1972 to $79.1 billion in 1981, equal to an annual growth rate of 50 percent during the period. Meanwhile, the share of official debt from the total debt declined from 45 percent in 1972 to 34 percent in 1981 (see Table 2-1). A relative decline in the annual official debt is also reflected in a comparison of the average annual growth rate of official debt (36 percent) versus the average annual growth rate of private debt (62 percent) in the 1972-81 period. This means that official lenders became relatively less active in financing LDCs in that period.

The annual changes in the components of official debt over time are given in Tables 2-2 and 2-3. The data in Table 2-2 indicate that the decline of official debt is attributed mainly to bilateral loans. The share of annual bilateral loans from the total official loans declined from 73 percent in 1972 and 86 percent in 1973 to 60 percent in 1981. Note that within bilateral loans, the share of concessional loans, particularly of DAC members, substantially declined over time. The share of concessional bilateral loans decreased from 53 percent in 1972 and 64 percent in 1973 to 39 percent in 1979. This striking decline is basically due to a lesser degree of participation on the part of DAC members, whose share of concessional loans dropped from 41 percent in 1972 and 49 percent in 1973 to 27 percent in 1979 (see Table 2-2).

A part of the relative decline in the concessional loans of DAC members has been offset by the increasing concessional loans of OPEC members, particularly between 1974 and 1976. In 1975, for instance, 18 percent of the total annual official loans were granted by OPEC members. However, the increasing share of the latter group was temporary, as

TABLE 2-1. Annual Official and Private Debt Inflow (Disbursed) to LDCs (billions of U.S. dollars)

	1972	1974	1976	1977	1978	1979	1980	1981	Growth Annual (1972-81)
Official debt (disbursed)	6.4	10.8	14.4	17.0	19.1	22.0	27.3	27.7	36%
Portion of total debt	45%	43%	37%	35%	29%	29%	38%	34%	
Private debt (disbursed)	7.9	14.2	23.9	30.3	45.7	52.8	44.7	51.8	62%
Portion of total debt	55%	57%	63%	65%	71%	71%	62%	66%	
Total official and private debt	14.3	25.0	38.3	47.3	64.8	74.8	72.0	79.1	50%

Source: World Debt Tables.

20

OPEC members were faced later with the erosion of their surpluses. As Table 2–2 suggests, in 1972 only 1 percent of the official loans were financed by concessional OPEC loans. The corresponding share reached a peak of 18 percent in 1975 and then plummeted to 6 percent in 1979. The concessional loans of the centrally planned economies also declined, from 10 percent in 1972 and 1973 to 5 percent in 1979. With respect to nonconcessional bilateral loans, the shares of all lenders, except for OPEC members, remained relatively unchanged during that period. Meanwhile, the share of the nonconcessional loans of OPEC members rose from 1 percent in 1972 to 4 percent in 1979.

A relative decline in bilateral loans in general, and in DAC concessional loans in particular, could be attributed to three factors: an increasing role of multilateral official lenders, an increasing role of private institutions in financing LDCs, and a general recession in DAC countries. The following will further justify these interpretations.

Table 2–3 is indicative of the fact that multilateral loans, in the category of official loans, became more and more important in the 1970s and 1980s. While bilateral loans declined in that period, the share of multilateral loans from the total official loans continuously increased, from 26 percent in 1972 to 40 percent in 1981 (see Table 2–3). This trend is true for the shares of both concessional and nonconcessional multilateral loans in that period. This means that international institutions (World Bank group and regional banks and institutions) became relatively more involved in financing the official debt of LDCs as the relative share of DAC lenders diminished over time.

Within the category of multilateral loans, the increasing role of regional banks and institutions is even more impressive. Their share of concessional and nonconcessional loans rose from 1 percent and 3 percent in 1972 to 7 percent and 6 percent in 1979, respectively. Note that the share of concessional loans of the regional banks and institutions has even surpassed that of World Bank group since 1977. However, the share of nonconcessional loans of the World Bank group remained dominant in the category of official loans and even slightly increased over time.

In summary, the annual inflow of multilateral debt had an increasing share in the 1970s. This increase basically stemmed from an increasing role of regional banks and institutions in financing both concessional and nonconcessional loans and a mild increase in the relative share of the World Bank group, particularly in nonconcessional loans.

As a policy, DAC countries have periodically set a financing target requiring each industrial country to con-

TABLE 2-2. Annual Bilateral Debt Inflow (Disbursed) to LDCs (millions of U.S. dollars)

	1972	1973	1974	1975	1976	1977	1978	1979	1980	1981
Total bilateral debt (disbursed)	5,450 73%	6,385 86%	8,000 71%	10,985 71%	10,219 67%	10,506 60%	11,914 61%	13,052 61%	16,565 60%	16,741 60%
Concessional	3,967 53%	4,759 64%	5,734 51%	8,165 53%	7,035 46%	7,185 41%	7,913 40%	8,363 39%	N/A	N/A
DAC	3,044 41%	3,641 49%	3,845 34%	4,467 29%	4,420 29%	4,343 25%	5,602 28%	5,772 27%		
OPEC	64 1%	265 3%	1,106 9%	2,813 18%	1,691 11%	1,459 8%	1,076 5%	1,351 6%		
Centrally planned economies	795 10%	770 10%	655 5%	691 4%	790 5%	1,240 7%	1,088 5%	1,133 5%		
Other	61.7 1%	82 1%	127 1%	192 1%	132 1%	142 1%	145 1%	106 1%		
Nonconcessional	1,483 20%	1,626 21%	2,266 20%	2,820 18%	3,184 21%	3,321 19%	4,001 20%	4,689 22%	N/A	N/A
DAC	1,252 16%	1,452 19%	1,742 15%	2,118 13%	2,357 15%	2,295 13%	2,925 15%	3,345 15%		

22

	C1	C2	C3	C4	C5	C6	C7	C8	C9	C10
OPEC	65 1%	22 0%	190 1%	351 2%	467 3%	662 3%	566 3%	802 4%		
Centrally planned economies	66 1%	46 1%	121 1%	166 1%	115 0%	96 0%	144 1%	259 1%		
Other	100 1%	100 1%	213 1%	185 1%	245 1%	268 1%	366 1%	283 1%		
Total official debt (disbursed)	7,411	8,826	11,237	15,371	15,108	17,269	19,485	21,234	27,399	27,752

Note: All percentages are expressed as of the total official debt (disbursed).
Source: World Bank, World Debt Tables.

TABLE 2-3. Annual Multilateral Debt Inflow (Disbursed) to LDCs (millions of U.S. dollars)

	1972	1973	1974	1975	1976	1977	1978	1979	1980	1981
Total multilateral debt (disbursed)	1,961	2,441	3,237	4,386	4,889	6,763	7,571	8,182	10,834	11,011
	26%	27%	28%	28%	32%	39%	38%	38%	39%	40%
Concessional	485	843	1,118	1,467	1,758	3,022	3,296	2,934	N/A	N/A
	6%	9%	9%	9%	11%	17%	16%	13%		
World Bank group	377	682	873	1,123	1,336	1,123	1,051	1,397		
	5%	7%	7%	7%	8%	6%	5%	6%		
Regional banks and institutions	108	161	245	344	422	1,899	2,245	1.537		
	1%	1%	2%	2%	2%	10%	11%	7%		
Nonconcessional	1,476	1,598	2,119	2,919	3,131	3,741	4,275	5,248	N/A	N/A
	19%	18%	18%	18%	20%	21%	21%	24%		
World Bank group	1,185	1,197	1,580	2,110	2,193	2,490	2,913	3,849		
	15%	13%	14%	13%	14%	14%	14%	18%		
Regional banks and institutions	291	401	539	809	938	1,251	1,362	1,399		
	3%	4%	4%	5%	6%	7%	6%	6%		
Total official debt (disbursed)	7,411	8,826	11,237	15,371	15,108	17,269	19,485	21,234	27,399	27,752

Source: World Bank, World Debt Tables.

tribute a certain percentage of its GDP to the Official Development Assistance (ODA) of LDCs. However, various reports of UNCTAD (United Nations Conference on Trade and Development) suggest that only a few countries have met the ODA targets. The industrialized nations in turn argue that the rising cost of imported energy, the difficulties in their balance of payments, the scarcity of credit, and more alternative sources of finance for LDCs have justified the diminishing of their traditional share of bilateral official loans.

Although international institutions, which have been involved in multilateral loans, offset part of the decline in official loans, one must remember that the lending capacity of these institutions has been limited. For instance, it has often been argued that the World Bank is not a full-fledged bank. The World Bank is not in a position to convert funds from one form to another and roll over short-term deposits like a commercial bank does. Also, its long process of evaluating and selecting projects has often been criticized by borrowing LDCs, which may need a certain amount of funds for a certain purpose and at a certain time. The concessional values of multilateral loans could potentially be offset by various restrictive clauses, such as using funds in specific areas and/or in a specific time period. The lending capacity of multilateral lenders such as the World Bank is further limited by the fact that prospective depositors may view the assets of the Bank as a semipolitically diversified portfolio that is not constructed in a way to minimize risk for a certain rate of return. Thus the World Bank cannot offer its debt instruments competitively in the market to broaden its resources to serve the needs of LDCs.

All this suggests that although the role of multilateral lenders did increase in the 1970s, their potential services have been constrained. This, coupled with a striking decline in bilateral official loans, is among the reasons for a major shift by LDCs to private borrowing, the trend of which will be reviewed in the following discussion.

As previously stated, the annual private debt disbursed to LDCs had a spectacular annual growth rate of 62 percent in 1972–81. In 1980 and 1981, private debt constituted 62 and 66 percent of the total debt inflow to LDCs, respectively (see Table 2–1). With respect to debt outstanding and disbursed (the stock of debt), the share of private debt also increased from 26 percent of the total debt in 1972 to 43 percent in 1981 (see Table 2–4). Note that the share of private debt in outstanding terms in Table 2–4 is less impressive than that of the annual private debt dis-

TABLE 2-4. Official and Private Debt Outstanding and Disbursed of LDCs (billions of U.S. dollars)

	1972	1974	1976	1977	1978	1979	1980	1981
Official debt	44	61	83	99	118	134	154	168
	49%	45%	43%	41%	40%	38%	38%	36%
Private debt	23	42	71	93	125	154	176	199
	26%	31%	36%	39%	42%	43%	44%	43%
Suppliers	8	11	14	17	20	21	21	19
	8%	8%	7%	7%	7%	6%	5%	4%
Financial markets	14	29	54	74	103	132	154	179
	15%	21%	27%	30%	34%	37%	38%	39%
Private debt/nonguaranteed	22	32	40	46	54	63	73	93
	25%	24%	21%	19%	18%	18%	18%	20%
Total official and private	90	135	195	240	298	352	404	461
	100%	100%	100%	100%	100%	100%	100%	100%

Source: World Bank, World Debt Tables.

bursement in Table 2–1. This is because the aggressive inflow of private debt to LDCs, relative to the inflow of official debt, is a new phenomenon. However, the share of accumulated private debt (outstanding and disbursed) has continuously risen since 1972; conversely, the corresponding share of accumulated official debt (outstanding and disbursed) has continuously declined (see Table 2–4).

As regards the components of private debt, the share of financial markets (guaranteed) has been very impressive. In 1972, only 15 percent of total debt outstanding and disbursed were supplied by financial markets, whereas the corresponding ratio increased to 39 percent in 1981. Thus the loans of private financial institutions, which mainly consist of Eurocredits, were a main source of LDC financing in 1972–81. In the light of such trends, some explanations about the rising share of private borrowing and Eurocredits in financing of LDCs are in order.

Citing any specific year in the 1970s as the start of aggressive private borrowing by LDCs is less than accurate. Neither the trend of annual inflows of debt to LDCs (Table 2–1) nor the trend of outstanding and disbursed debt (Table 2–4) can provide a clear-cut year in this regard. Thus it is more accurate to refer to the mid-1970s rather than a single year as the time when LDCs made a major shift, in aggregated terms, to private lending sources.

This shift is concurrent with a major transfer of income from industrialized countries and oil-importing LDCs to OPEC members. As a result of the latter transfer of income, mainly due to rising prices of imported oil, the oil-importing LDCs and members of OECD ran into spectacular current account deficits. Meanwhile, the surplus counterparts of the above deficits were exorbitant for OPEC countries.* The OPEC surplus, which could not totally and immediately be absorbed by the OPEC economies, became a new source of borrowing in the form of deposits with private banks in international financial markets.

At this juncture, the LDCs that were in deficit had to contend with the impact of recession and the deflationary policies of the industrialized countries, on the one hand, and to adjust their economies to the rise in costs of imported oil and other related commodities, on the other. The implication of the former was less availability of official

---

*The surplus of OPEC countries was estimated to be more than $43 billion in 1974. Meantime, the OECD countries had a deficit of more than $19 billion.

loans and, in particular, concessional loans from DAC members. The implication of the latter differed from one group of LDCs to another. The LDCs, generally of middle income and particularly of industrialized economies, such as Korea, Brazil, and Mexico, had access to the international private financial institutions that were recycling OPEC surpluses to the deficit countries. While this group of LDCs could afford to finance their imports and continue their growth policies, many other LDCs either had difficulty in obtaining access to private lenders or preferred to remain the beneficiaries of traditional official loans. As of the end of 1980, nine LDCs (Brazil, Mexico, Venezuela, Argentina, Korea, the Philippines, Algeria, Chile, and Indonesia) maintained 64 percent of the outstanding and disbursed loans of the private banks. The concentration of private debt in the LDCs is more understood as one notices that 77 LDCs received only about 20 percent of the total private banks' credits.[b]

An important point to mention is that the rise of private borrowing of LDCs should not be attributed exclusively to the emergence of the OPEC surplus in the mid-1970s. The fact that the private debt of LDCs was rising even when the OPEC surplus was failing suggests that the OPEC surplus and the theory of "recycling" is not a comprehensive explanation of the phenomenon. The U.S. current deficits, as well as the European intervention to support currencies, tend to increase the supply of dollars that may eventually enter the Euromarket system and be used as Eurocredits to the borrowers, including LDCs. Besides, a slower economic activity in the industrialized countries may reduce the demand for domestic loans. If, meanwhile, the banks in those industrialized countries have surplus loanable funds, they may take a more active role in offering loans in international markets where a group of LDCs is demanding foreign loans. All this, coupled with the particular characteristics of international private banks (Eurobanks)—including the flexibility of their interest rates, the speed of negotiations and transactions, the option for repayment of debt before maturity, and the freedom of using borrowed funds (unlike in most cases of official loans)—are plausible explanations for the rise of private LDC borrowing in the 1970s and 1980s.

As previously stated, Eurocredits have been the dominant type of private loan to LDCs. Table 2-5 gives the trend and the size of Eurocredits to LDCs from 1972 to 1982. According to Table 2-4, the year 1973, with a spectacular growth rate of 189 percent, was the start of aggressive borrowing from the Euromarket by LDCs. This significant growth remained steady with an annual growth rate of 22 to 42 percent from 1974 to 1978. While the market was relatively stagnant in 1979, the annual growth rate of LDC borrowing was 16 percent. Thus the Euro-credit market was systematically used by borrowing LDCs throughout 1973–79. Various reports of the Bank for International Settlements indicate more than 50 percent of the total Eurocredits was used by the borrowing LDCs in the second half of the 1970s.

Table 2–5 reveals that the pace of the LDC borrowings slowed down in 1980–82 with annual growth rates of 7, 2, and -29 percent, respectively. In view of the increasing payment difficulties of a few large borrowing countries, such as Mexico, Brazil, and Argentina, the latest decline in the rate of LDC borrowing is not surprising. After various forms of debt rescheduling in 1981–82, these countries could not afford to borrow significant funds form private financial markets.

The last category of loans to LDCs is the bond markets, which consist of Eurobonds and foreign bonds. Table 2–6 indicates that the share of LDC borrowing from the Euro-bond market increased from 3 percent in 1974 to 19 percent in 1979. Thereafter, the corresponding share declined and remained stationary. The share of LDC borrowing from the foreign bonds market remained relatively constant, below 10 percent, throughout the 1970s. The ratio significantly declined in the 1980s and reached as low as 2 percent in 1982–83.

In fact, the major portion of the LDC bond issues was make by only a few upper-middle-income LDCs, such as Mexico, Brazil, Korea, Venezuela, and Spain. A declining share, or at best a constant share, of LDC borrowing from the bond markets suggests that this market constituted very limited and unsystematic sources of loans for LDCs in the 1970s and the 1980s. This limitation can be explained by the attitude of prospective private lenders toward the LDC bonds and the rigidity of government regulations and disclosure requirements in the market country.

With respect to the attitude of private lenders, LDC bonds may be associated with two elements of risk. One is political and the other is economic.[7] A change in govern-ment, in the case of a long-term investment in an LDC bond, could be a possible political risk from the viewpoint of a private investor. Besides, the ability of a developing economy to generate sufficient funds to repay the debt over a period of time is an economic risk that a risk averter may refuse to take. Thus an LDC bond issuer could be "crowd-ed out" if an established borrower, usually an industrial

TABLE 2-5. Growth Rates of Eurocurrency Funds Used by Borrowing LDCs, 1972-82 (billions of U.S. dollars)

	1972	1973	1974	1975	1976	1977	1978	1979	1980	1981	1982
Borrowing LDCs (except Eastern Europe)	3.8	11.0	15.7	19.5	24.7	30.3	40.1	46.9	50.1	51.0	36.0
Annual rate of growth		189%	42%	24%	26%	22%	32%	16%	7%	2%	-29%

Source: Bank for International Settlements, annual reports.

TABLE 2-6. International Bond Issues (millions of U.S. dollars)

	1974	1975	1976	1977	1978	1979	1980	1981	1982	1983*
Total Eurobond*	4,520	10,200	14,930	19,480	15,940	17,900	20,510	27,180	46,450	51,000
Share of the LDCs	140	470	1,040	2,660	2,990	1,830	1,180	2,300	2,820	N/A
	3%	5%	7%	14%	19%	10%	6%	8%	6%	N/A
Total foreign bonds*	7,790	11,830	18,010	16,610	21,380	19,180	18,930	21,580	25,200	32,480
Share of the LDCs	790	480	810	1,610	2,200	1,410	570	1,120	520	560
	10%	4%	4%	10%	10%	7%	3%	5%	2%	2%

*Eurobonds are denominated in a currency other than that of the borrowing country and offered in different markets. Foreign bonds are usually offered in a specific country and denominated in that country's currency.
Source: Bank for International Settlements, annual reports.

country, is simultaneously in the market. Government regulations as to the disclosure of information about the borrower have been another problem for the unsophisticated borrowing LDCs, which suffer from a poor system of national accounts and data. In the case of using the Euro-bond market, there are a series of procedural problems in the process of developing a bond issue prospectus.[8] These requirements might impede a number of LDCs from using the bond markets (foreign and international) to raise capital. The combination of all these factors constitutes a plausible explanation for a very limited share of the bond market in the total borrowing of LDCs.

Finally, a new development in financing LDCs is the rise of Arab bank lending. The value of Arab bank lending fluctuated from $1 billion to less that $3 billion in 1976–79, of which the annual share of loans to oil-importing LDCs fluctuated between 3 and 10 percent. The major receivers of Arab bank lending in that period were OPEC and OECD countries.[9] However, with the support of their governments, as the major shareholders, the Arab banks are in a position to expand their assets in the process of lending to LDCs. In 1982, more than one-third and two-thirds of Arab bank lending were allocated to oil-importing LDCs and all LDCs, respectively. This suggests that the loans from Arab banks are becoming an increasing source of finance for borrowing LDCs. The Arab Investment Company, which was set up in Riyadh, has already started its aggressive development lending to the private sector in the Middle East. Similarly, other institutions, in Abu Dhabi, Bahrain, and Kuwait, with a strong motivation to gain the profit of future recycling, have also become active in financing the regional borrowing LDCs.

CONCLUSION

The LDCs have aggressively borrowed from various sources in the 1970s and the 1980s. The loans of the LDCs can be categorized into official loans and private loans. Official loans included bilateral and multilateral financing provided on a concessional or nonconcessional basis. Private loans took the form of either suppliers' credits or borrowings from financial markets, such as the Eurocredit and Euro-bond markets.

In the category of official loans, the share of bilateral loans gradually declined and the share of multilateral loans continuously increased. Meantime, official loans were significantly outpaced by private loans. The phenomenal growth of private loans was attributed to the increasing share of the loans from the Eurocredit market. The portion of borrowings from the Eurobond market was minimal. In the 1980s, LDC borrowing from private sources has subsided because of the deteriorating debt position of many LDCs.

NOTES

1. *World Debt Tables,* EC-167/81 (Washington, D.C.: World Bank, 1981), p. iii.
2. Ibid., p. iv.
3. See "Cost and Benefits of Aids: An Empirical Analysis," in *Leading Issues in Economic Development,* ed. Gerald M. Meier (New York: Oxford University Press, 1976), pp. 345–46.
4. With a caveat that the term Eurodollar could be misleading, a Eurodollar is a U.S. dollar deposited outside the United States (in Europe or elsewhere). A Eurocurrency, in general, is a national currency deposited outside the national boundary. For a basic description of the Eurocurrency markets, see R. Rodriguez and E. Carter, *International Financial Management* (Englewood Cliffs, N.J.: Prentice Hall, 1979), chap. 13.
5. The Eurofinancial markets consist mainly of the Eurocurrency market, the Eurocredit market, and the Eurobond market. The Eurocurrency market is a short-term money market in which banks borrow short-term deposits from one another. The Eurocredit market, originally established for medium-term loans, now offers both medium- and long-term loans to various borrowers. The Eurobond market provides long-term loans, through issuing bonds simultaneously in various markets. See Yoon S. Park, "Background Briefing: Structure and Function of the Eurocredit Market," *Euromoney* (April 1974): 77–81. For details of the Eurocredit market, see Abtahi Saeed, "Financial Flows to the Developing Countries: The Case of Eurodollar Credit" (D.B.A. dissertation, Harvard University, 1976).
6. Richard O'Brian, *Private Bank Lending to Developing Countries,* Working Paper no. 482 (Washington, D.C.: World Bank, August 1981), Table 2, p. 3.
7. Robert G. Hawkins et al., *Improving the Access of Developing Countries to the U.S. Capital Market* (New York: New York University Press, 1975), p. 38.
8. See Yoon S. Park, *The Eurobond Market Function and Structure* (New York: Praeger, 1974), pp. 37–40.

9. For a report on Arab Bank lending, see "Arab Banking," *Middle East Economic Digest,* Special Report (August 1981). See also O'Brian, *Private Bank Lending to Developing Countries,* pp. 44–46.

3
Results
of Empirical Analysis

The purposes of this chapter are to report the derived data, determine the paired borrowing countries, calculate the annual values of growth indicators for each country in each pair, execute the paired t-tests and multiple regressions, organize and interpret the results, answer the major question of the research, and, finally, evaluate the validity of the research hypothesis.

Table 3–1 is the summary result of steps 1 to 4 of the methodology section as described in Chapter 1. The objective is to identify the borrowing countries whose monetary values of direct investment have been close (or insignificantly different) in the borrowing period under study. The fulfillment of this condition, which helps minimize the effect of equity inflow, is also verified by the paired t-tests. In Table 3–1 the average monetary values of direct investment, adjusted for size, have been calculated for the period 1963–77, as well as for the five-year periods of 1963–67, 1968–72, and 1973–77. The average values of the short intervals (five-year periods) indicate whether the similarity of equity inflow has been consistently true for the entire period. Similar calculations have been done for the debt inflow to the sample countries in Table 3–2, the summary result of steps 5 to 8 in the methodology section. Average monetary values of debt inflow to individual countries are determined for the period 1963–77, as well as for the five-year periods of 1963–67, 1968–72, and 1973–77.

TABLE 3-1. Average Annual Values of Direct Investment Adjusted for Size of Economy--A Summary

		Average Annual Values	Average Annual Values in Short Periods		
Rank	Country	1963-77	1963-67	1968-72	1973-77
1	Jamaica*	.06775	.07279	.13588	.00820
2	Cyprus	.03740	N/A	N/A	.04056
3	Malaysia	.02799	.02874	.01568	.03710
4	Costa Rica	.02525	N/A	N/A	.02610
5	Ecuador*	.02156	.00879	.04871	.01261
6	Tunisia*	.01869	.02384	.01378	.01859
7	Paraguay*	.01785	.02012	.01652	.01692
8	Dominican Republic	.01646	N/A	N/A	.01975
9	Guatemala*	.01484	.01572	.01771	.01160
10	Panama*	.01239	.01266	.01623	.00904
11	Brazil	.00725	.00440	.00576	.01013
12	Portugal*	.00596	.00853	.00471	.00465
13	Peru*	.00561	.00757	.00357	.00487
14	Colombia*	.00462	.00678	.00466	.00403
15	Jordan	.00250	.00208	.00180	.00383
16	Turkey	.00246	.00245	.00187	.00309
17	Mexico	.00174	(.00670)	.00420	.00826
18	Korea	.00167	(.00037)	.00123	.00407
19	Argentina	.00152	.00123	.00007	.00337
20	Chile*	(.00355)	.00254	(.00363)	(.00837)

*The average annual values of direct investment, adjusted for size of economy, declined for this country in the third period compared to the first and/or the second period(s).

Source: Based on the procedure specified in the methodology section in Chapter 1.

In Tables 3–1 and 3–2 countries are ranked according to their levels of direct investment and levels of debt inflow, adjusted for size, for 1963–77. For instance, Jamaica, Cyprus, Malaysia, Costa Rica, and Ecuador are among the top receivers of equity capital, after adjustment for the size of their economies. With regard to the level of debt capital inflow, Table 3–2 reveals that Tunisia, Panama, Korea, Costa Rica, Jamaica, and Peru are among the top borrowers, relative to the size of their economies. Obviously,

TABLE 3-2. Average Annual Values of External Borrowing Adjusted for Size of Economy--A Summary

Rank	Country	Average Annual Values 1963-77	Average Annual Values in Short Periods		
			1963-67	1968-72	1973-77
1	Tunisia	.07091	.08171	.06685	.06417
2	Panama*	.06829	.01899	.04760	.13827
3	Korea*	.05674	.02456	.07355	.07211
4	Costa Rica*	.04708	.03789	.03929	.06407
5	Jamaica*	.04613	.02779	.03138	.07922
6	Peru*	.04463	.02968	.02819	.07601
7	Mexico*	.03768	.02742	.02485	.06077
8	Chile*	.03581	N/A	.03435	.03841
9	Jordan*	.03285	.02296	.00564	.09551
10	Paraguay	.02530	.02264	.03204	.02122
11	Brazil*	.02376	.01207	.01980	.03147
12	Malaysia*	.01903	.01351	.01774	.02474
13	Cyprus	.01861	.01184	.01146	.03252
14	Portugal*	.01857	.02847	.01090	.01635
15	Turkey	.01818	.01571	.01479	.01163
16	Argentina*	.01675	.01589	.02479	.02111
17	Guatemala	.01342	.01406	.01494	.01126
18	Colombia*	.01178	.00309	.00491	.02735
19	Dominican Republic	.01082	.00271	.00267	.02543
20	Ecuador	.00836	.00836	.00874	.00832

*The average annual values of external borrowing, adjusted for size of economy, increased for this country in the third period compared to the first and/or the second period(s).

Source: Based on the procedure specified in the methodology section in Chapter 1.

this ranking does not reflect the absolute values of external borrowing, as the values of borrowing have been divided by gross domestic product for further comparative analysis. Tables 3–1 and 3–2 provide the basis for pairing countries that have similar levels of equity capital and different levels of debt inflow. Before proceeding with the pairing process, some important observations from Tables 3–1 and 3–2 are discussed in the following section.

A DECLINING EQUITY INFLOW VERSUS
A RISING DEBT INFLOW

Table 3–1 reveals that the values of direct investment over GDP for a number of countries have declined in recent periods, whereas the corresponding values of debt inflow, for the majority of countries in Table 3–2, have increased in the same periods. Some examples are as follows: The average values of direct investment over GDP from the first five years (1963–67) to the third five years (1973–77) declined from .0729 to .00820 for Jamaica, from .02384 to .01859 for Tunisia, from .02012 to .01692 for Paraguay, from .01266 to .00904 for Panama, from .00853 to .00465 for Portugal, from .00757 to .00487 for Peru, and from a negative .00355 to a further negative of .00837 for Chile.

The reverse trend is true for debt inflow to most of the countries in the sample. For instance, the ratio for Panama increased from .01899 in the first five years to .04760 in the second five years and still further to .13827 in the third five years. The ratio for Korea increased from .02456 in the first five years to .07211 in the third five years. The ratio for Costa Rica increased from .03789 in the first five years to .06407 in the third five years. The ratio for Peru increased from .02968 in the first five years to .07601 in the third five years. Similar trends exist for some of the other countries.

Except for the giant LDCs, such as Korea, Mexico, and Brazil, a decreasing trend in equity capital inflow and an increasing trend in debt capital inflow seem to be the pattern for many LDCs. A partial explanation for this phenomenon is disinvestment (or divestments) on the part of multinationals due to a variety of political reasons. There were at least 1,004 cases of disinvestment of foreign operations in 1972–75, of which a sizable portion was in LDCs.[1] For Latin American countries, from which most of the sample is taken, the ratio of disinvestments to the total number of disinvestments increased from 18 percent in 1967 to 43 percent in 1971. In 1972–75, the divestments of operations in mineral resources, petroleum exploration and refining, and agriculture in LDCs accounted for two-thirds of all nationalizations and expropriations.[2]

The specific cases in the following discussion support the interpretation that disinvestment has been a cause of a relative reduction of foreign ownership compared to foreign debt in some LDCs.

Following the Marxist socialism of Allende (1970–73), the strategy of the Pinochet government was to attract more direct investment into the Chilean economy. The objective was to bridge the widening gap between very low indigenous capital sources and the required investment expenditures for the target economic growth. The Foreign Investment Statute of July 1974 focused on foreign equity as the major solution to the short- and medium-term capital shortage in the country.[3] The government immediately started to arrange negotiation for outstanding expropriation claims carried form the previous regime. A foreign investment provision for equal treatment of local and foreign business entities, along with relaxed remittance policies, was enacted promptly. Special decrees were put into effect to give preferential treatment for tax purposes to international businesses operating in Chile. The government also set up a special committee to process the applications of foreign companies efficiently and to notify them of the results promptly—a response to the bureaucracy problem that had existed for years in the government sector of Chile. The committee became the only channel of communication between prospective foreign investors and the decision makers in the government.

During 1974–78, the committee effectively processed numerous applications, of which 319 projects were approved. These projects were supposed to attract an inflow of U.S. $2.5 billion to the financially stressed economy of Chile. However, only 20 percent of the accepted projects entered the country.[4]

As calculations in Table 3–1 reveal, there was a negative net inflow of equity capital into Chile during 1973–77. A plausible explanation is that the "involuntary" disinvestments of the previous regime created such a paranoid attitude among foreign investors that they adopted a wait-and-see strategy rather than giving a quick response even to the invitation of the new pro-business government of Pinochet. Furthermore, Chile still had some obligation to follow some of the deterrent regulations of the Andean Pact.[5] (According to the Andean Pact a foreign company has an obligation to transfer the ownership and management control to local entities after a certain period of time.)

The negative values of direct investment before 1974 must be related to the attitude of the previous regime toward foreign business. It is appropriate to mention that the Marxist socialism of Allende was unequivocal about its strategy toward foreign investments. The main strategy of the Allende government was to restructure the economy through state planning, state ownership, and state control. Nationalization of the major industries, the first item on any Marxist-Leninist revolutionary economic agenda, led to "involuntary disinvestments" and subsequently caused a negative ratio of direct investment over GDP. The relatively favorable ratio of direct investment over GDP in the first five years (1963–67) in Table 3–1 can be partially explained by the moderate political position of Christian Democracy under Feri (1964–70), which encouraged the operation of foreign entities in Chile. A very lucrative market for copper in the mid-1960s, coupled with the favorable attitude of the government, is among the reasons for the positive values of direct investment in this period.

The case of Portugal, although less serious than that of Chile, is another example of a diminishing ratio of direct investment over GDP. The average ratio in the third five years (1973–77) is even less than half of the average ratio in the first five years (1963–67). The five years preceding the revolution of 1974 were characterized by relatively high rates of foreign direct investment. The ratio sharply declined in the latter periods (see Table 3–1). These findings are also consistent with the World Bank report that the gross fixed capital formation of almost all export sectors, which previously had a major equity participation of foreign investors, declined sharply immediately after the revolution.[6]

Despite the fact that the revolutionary regime in Portugal was much more moderate and pragmatic than that in Chile, the new government nationalized all banking and insurance institutions, power companies, the major transportation agencies, and the large industrial groups. However, unlike the revolutionary regime of Allende, the revolutionary government in Portugal delineated the line between public and private sectors. In late 1975, the government announced the criteria for compensation of previously expropriated assets and promised no further nationalization. Private enterprises were officially permitted to participate in all sectors except military items, oil, petrochemicals, fertilizer, iron and steel, cement, water, power, telecommunications, and public transport.[7] Despite all these encouraging actions, the Portuguese government could not reverse the trend of reduced direct investment, at least before the end of the third five-year period (1973–77).

Trade union activity in the form of a new radical codetermination, higher minimum wages that were incompatible with the low productivity of labor and low efficiency of the economy after the revolution, and new unemployment and social security benefits were all new to foreign investors. Compounded with all this is the fact that the revolution of Portugal occurred exactly at the time that the world economy was in a very bad recession. The increasing price of oil, the slackening demand for the export items of Portugal, a general recession, and the revolution—all concurrently deterred expansion of foreign direct investment in Portugal in the third period.

With regard to the case of Peru, the sharp reduction of direct investment over GDP in the second five years (1967–72) can be partially attributed to the ethnocentric view of the new regime in 1968. This, coupled with the pressure of the national bourgeoise, led to further control of the major industries and tougher terms on which foreign investors could operate in Peru. The new government of General Velasco expropriated some of the major foreign enterprises that previously had been operating in a laissez-faire framework. [8]

In contrast to the relative decline of equity inflow to LDCs, the data in Table 3–2 reveal that debt inflow was on the rise for most of the sample countries in the second and/or third five-years period(s). The average ratios of debt over GDP in the third five-year period were higher than those of the first five-year and/or the second five-year period(s) for Panama, Korea, Costa Rica, Jamaica, Peru, Mexico, Chile, Jordan, Brazil, Malaysia, Cyprus, Portugal, Argentina, and Colombia. A plausible explanation for the increasing debt is the more active role of public and private international financial institutions in the latter years. As discussed in Chapter 2, the volume of private loans, as well as multilateral and bilateral loans, including the official loans from OPEC countries to LDCs, all increased during the period under study. In particular, the aggressive banking of private institutions, even in some less creditworthy countries, explains the continuous increase of debt to LDCs in the 1970s.

In the era of a relative decline of foreign investment (foreign ownership), LDCs had to shift to more borrowing to bridge the widening gap between their domestic savings and investment expenditures. Despite political instability in many LDCs, a good number of these countries were pursuing relatively high targets of economic growth. For example, from the early 1960s to 1974 there was a continuous rate of increase in the ratio of investment over GDP in 14 countries in Latin America—more than 25 percent in Ecuador, Jamaica, and Panama and more than 20 percent in Argentina, Brazil, Costa Rica, Dominican Republic, Mexico, Paraguay, and Peru. [9] These investment expenditures obviously required an extensive foreign capital inflow either through debt or equity.

In view of a declining share of equity inflow on the one hand and the increasing role of financial agencies on the other, debt inflow became the dominant source of capital to fill the internal gap (investment minus savings) or the external gap (export minus import) of LDCs in the 1970s. Therefore LDCs became more and more aggressive in borrowing in the 1970s. Although the portion of official flows compared to private flows to LDCs has declined in recent years, the combined lending by the World Bank group (IBRD, IDA, and IFC) and the Inter-American Development Bank exceeded $12 billion by the end of 1978[10]—equal to an annual rate of 32 percent increase over a previous year. The increase in official multilateral loans becomes much higher when loans from other institutions, such as the Asian Development Bank and the African Development Bank, are included.

In summary, based on the observation and interpretation of the data in Tables 3–1 and 3–2, the author tends to believe that the inflow of external debt outpaced the inflow of foreign equity for a number of LDCs in the 1970s.

PAIRING PROCESS: A HIGH-BORROWING COUNTRY VERSUS A LOW-BORROWING COUNTRY

From Tables 3–1 and 3–2 the following seven pairs of countries, which meet the criteria set in the methodology section, were selected:

High Borrowing	Low Borrowing
Costa Rica	Ecuador
Tunisia	Paraguay
Panama	Guatemala
Peru	Portugal
Peru	Colombia
Chile	Argentina
Korea	Mexico

The countries in each pair have the following characteristics:

- The average monetary values of direct investment over GDP of the two countries in each pair are similar. This condition is verified by paired t-tests in Table 3–3.
- The average monetary values of direct investment over GDP of the two countries in each pair remain close in every five-year period.
- The average monetary values of debt over GDP of the two countries in each pair are significantly different, as verified by the paired t-tests in Table 3–3.

Debt inflow over GDP of the two countries in each pair has the most possible different average values in the sample. As verified by paired t-tests in Table 3–3, the average monetary values of debt over GDP for the two countries in each pair are all significantly different at a confidence level of 99 percent. The confidence level for Korea versus Mexico is 95 percent.

It is important to mention that the dichotomy of high borrowing versus low borrowing used in this study is a relative concept. For instance, the economy of Costa Rica, with an annual average of external debt inflow about 5 percent of GDP, is considered a high-borrowing country compared to Ecuador, whose annual debt over GDP was only .86 percent in the same period of study. Also, the effect of adjustment for size (debt over GDP and direct investment over GDP) led to a few striking results (see Tables 3–1 and 3–2). For instance, Tunisia, with more than 7 percent of annual debt/GDP in 1963 to 1977, is ranked higher than even a giant borrower like Korea, with an annual ratio of 5.6 percent in the same period. However, in the pairing process the author has been careful not to pair, for instance, a giant LDC like Mexico with a country like Colombia merely because they have similar values of direct investment over GDP and different values of debt over GDP. After time-consuming trial and error, it was determined that the chosen pairs were the best possible pairs of countries from the primary sample that were in agreement with the selection criteria.

ANSWERING THE MAJOR QUESTION OF THE RESEARCH

This section deals with the statistical interpretation of the paired t-tests and the multiple regressions to provide an answer to the major question raised in Chapter 1: Between two countries with similar equity capital inflow but different levels of external borrowing, did the country with a higher level of external borrowing maintain more variable growth indicators during a specified borrowing period? With the list of paired countries in Table 3–3, the annual values of the economic indicators were calculated for the countries in each pair. Table 3–4 is the summary result of this empirical analysis.

In explanation of the results, the reader should keep the following concepts in mind: Between two borrowing countries in a pair, the one with a *lower positive value* of incremental capital output ratio (ICOR) maintains a more

TABLE 3-3. A High-Borrowing Country versus a Low-Borrowing Country: Average Annual Values of External Borrowing and Direct Investment, Adjusted for Size of Economy, 1963-77

Paired Countries	External Borrowing, GDP	t-Ratio	Degrees of Freedom	Direct Investment, GDP	t-Ratio	Degrees of Freedom
Costa Rica Ecuador	.04708 .00836	5.25	14	.02525 .02156	1.08	5
Tunisia Paraguay	.07091 .02530	6.09	14	.01869 .01785	.27	14
Panama Guatemala	.06829 .01342	3.33	14	.01239 .01484	.18	13
Peru Portugal	.04463 .01857	3.77	14	.00561 .00596	1.51	11
Peru Colombia	.04463 .01178	7.80	14	.00561 .00462	1.37	11
Chile Argentina	.03581 .01675	6.30	14	(.00355) .00152	1.36	13
Korea Mexico	.05674 .03768	2.40	14	.00167 .00174	.04	13

Notes: The countries have been paired based on the procedure specified in the methodology section in Chapter 1. The average annual values of external borrowing divided by GDP in each pair are significantly different at a level of 99 percent. For the case of Korea versus Mexico, the confidence level is 95 percent. A confidence level of 95 percent has been used as a basis to determine that the two countries in each pair have insignificantly different average annual values of direct investment divided by GDP.

44

TABLE 3-4. Average Annual Values of Macroeconomic Indicators for High-Borrowing versus Low-Borrowing Countries, 1965-79

High Borrowing versus Low Borrowing	Incremental Capital Output Ratio		Marginal Savings Ratio		Average Savings Ratio		Growth Rate of Export	
	Mean	t-Ratio	Mean	t-Ratio	Mean	t-Ratio	Mean	t-Ratio
Costa Rica	1.24	.18	.169	2.41*	.095	2.96*	.137	-.85
Ecuador	1.03	(DF=14)	.056	(DF=14)	.039	(DF=14)	.176	(DF=14)
Tunisia	2.14	1.95	.017	.17	.093	1.56	.198	1.05
Paraguay	1.31	(DF=14)	.015	(DF=14)	.084	(DF=14)	.126	(DF=14)
Panama	2.36	2.13	.198	-.93	.133	1.70	.096	-.90
Guatemala	1.56	(DF=14)	.209	(DF=12)	.101	(DF=11)	.144	(DF=14)
Peru	.66	-5.22*	.038	-5.19	.057	-3.69	.067	-.46
Portugal	1.24	(DF=14)	.561	(DF=12)	.373	(DF=13)	.115	(DF=14)
Peru	.66	-1.18	.038	-.80	.057	2.28*	.067	-.54
Colombia	.71	(DF=14)	.039	(DF=14)	.031	(DF=13)	.120	(DF=14)
Chile	N/A		.083	-5.32	.066	-7.36	.185	.502
Argentina			.197	(DF=8)	.180	(DF=6)	.123	(DF=12)
Korea	.60	-3.00*	.226	5.76*	.179	3.60*	.365	2.90*
Mexico	1.12	(DF=14)	.042	(DF=14)	.040	(DF=14)	.148	(DF=14)

45

TABLE 3-4. Continued

High-Borrowing versus Low-Borrowing	Growth Rate of GDP		Export/GDP		External Gap		Internal Gap	
	Mean	t-Ratio	Mean	t-Ratio	Mean	t-Ratio	Mean	t-Ratio
Costa Rica	.088	1.16	.230	2.41*	-.088	-3.21	-.116	.64
Ecuador	.080	(DF=14)	.190	(DF=14)	-.001	(DF=14)	-.151	(DF=14)
Tunisia	.067	.13	.138	1.03	-.111	-7.44	-.147	-3.18
Paraguay	.054	(DF=14)	.123	(DF=13)	-.002	(DF=14)	-.097	(DF=14)
Panama	.051	-1.35	.132	-2.66	-.252	-4.06	-.091	-1.08
Guatemala	.054	(DF=14)	.166	(DF=14)	-.012	(DF=14)	-.048	(DF=14)
Peru	.041	-1.43	.144	-.02	.004	3.21*	-.092	-3.82
Portugal	.051	(DF=14)	.161	(DF=13)	-.096	(DF=14)	.182	(DF=14)
Peru	.041	-1.45	.144	.83	.004	1.43	-.092	4.52*
Colombia	.056	(DF=14)	.117	(DF=13)	-.020	(DF=14)	-.152	(DF=14)
Chile	.069	1.21	.132	3.07*	.013	2.66*	N/A	
Argentina	.020	(DF=10)	.073	(DF=12)	-.011	(DF=12)		
Korea	.096	2.59*	.172	4.04*	-.098	-3.66	-.058	4.66*
Mexico	.059	(DF=14)	.050	(DF=14)	-.026	(DF=14)	-.162	(DF=14)

46

*Average annual difference has been significantly different, in favor of the high-borrowing country, at a confidence level of 95 percent.

Notes: The test hypotheses are as follows: Null hypothesis: average annual difference of a variable between a high-borrowing country and a low-borrowing country (the value for a high-borrowing country minus the value for a low-borrowing country) is equal to zero. Alternative hypothesis: average annual difference of a variable between a high-borrowing country and a low-borrowing country (the value for a high-borrowing country minus the value for a low-borrowing country) is greater than zero.

The weighted values of growth indicators have been used in computation of the t-ratios. That is, the annual values of growth indicators of the two countries in each pair have been weighted by the differences between the annual values of debt of the same countries.

favorable value of ICOR compared to the other. It is not very difficult to show that the negative values of ICOR are often misleading. Therefore the author decided from the outset to ignore any negative values of ICOR. With regard to other variables, *higher mathematical values* are indicative of more favorable performance of the economy. This is also true for the external gap and the internal gap, whose mathematical values, rather than their absolute values, have been incorporated in the calculations.

The value of the *t*-ratio for a specific variable could be positive or negative, depending on whether the average value of the economic indicator for the high-borrowing country is higher or lower than that of the low-borrowing country.* The interpretation of positive or negative values of *t*-ratio actually depends on the economic indicator itself. A significant *negative t-ratio* for ICOR tends to suggest that the high-borrowing country has had a more favorable ICOR on the average than that of a low-borrowing country, whereas for other variables significantly *positive t-ratios* tend to indicate that a high-borrowing country has maintained a more favorable performance in terms of those indicators. For instance, a negative *t*-ratio of 3 for the incremental capital output ratio of Korea versus Mexico in Table 3–4 means that the average annual difference of this ratio has been significantly more favorable (higher) for Korea at a confidence level of 99 percent, and a positive *t*-ratio of 5.76 for the marginal savings ratio tends to indicate that the average annual difference of this ratio has been significantly more favorable (higher) for Korea at the same level of confidence.

Tables 3–4 and 3–5 reveal that in only 16 of 56 tests executed was a high-borrowing country associated with more favorable values of macroeconomic indicators at a confidence level of 95 percent. Even at a lower confidence level of 90 percent, the result does not significantly improve. Leaving aside the case of Korea versus Mexico, only nine tests show significant differences between a high-borrowing country and a low-borrowing country in the sample.

Costa Rica versus Ecuador has maintained more favorable values in terms of only three variables of the eight variables studied. Tunisia versus Paraguay and Panama versus Guatemala have not held any higher (more favorable) values

---

*The formula for the *t*-test is basically as follows: $t = xd/sxd$, where xd is the mean difference and sxd is the standard error of the mean difference. Therefore t is positive if xd is positive, and vice versa.

TABLE 3-5. Pattern of Variables with Significantly Higher (More Favorable) Values

High Borrowing versus Low Borrowing	ICOR	Marginal Savings Ratio	Average Savings Ratio	Growth Rate of Export	Growth Rate of GDP	Export/ GDP	External Gap	Internal Gap
Costa Rica Ecuador		X	X			X		
Tunisia Paraguay								
Panama Guatemala								
Peru Portugal			X					X
Peru Colombia	X						X	
Chile Argentina						X	X	
Korea Mexico	X	X	X	X	X	X		X

Note: "X" indicates that the difference is significant at a 95 percent confidence level in favor of the high-borrowing country, as based on the results in Table 3-4.

49

in terms of any variables in the study. Peru, as a major borrower in the sample, was tested twice: first compared to Portugal and then compared to Colombia. In both cases, Peru has been associated with more favorable values in terms of only two variables. Chile versus Argentina has also held better values with respect to only two variables.

Furthermore, there is no consistency in terms of the variables in which the high-borrowing countries performed better than the low-borrowing countries. For instance, Costa Rica versus Ecuador has a more favorable performance in terms of the marginal savings ratio, the average savings ratio, and the export/GDP ratio, whereas Peru versus Portugal has a better performance in terms of the incremental capital output ratio and the external gap.

The results are more striking when one observes that in 25 instances the average values of the indicators of the high-borrowing countries are even less favorable compared to those of the low-borrowing countries. (Compare the values of the mean in Table 3–4, regardless of the test for the mean difference, between a high-borrowing country versus a low-borrowing country.) For instance, Peru has a lower value of the mean in terms of the marginal savings ratio, the average savings ratio, growth in export and GDP, the export/GDP ratio, and the internal gap compared to the corresponding values for Portugal. Compared to Colombia, Peru maintains lower values of the mean with respect to the marginal savings ratio and the growth rate of GDP.

Panama maintains less favorable average values in terms of the incremental capital output ratio, the growth rate of export, the growth rate of GDP, the external gap, and the internal gap compared to its paired low-borrowing country, Guatemala. Chile, another high-borrowing country, has lower values of the mean in terms of both the marginal savings ratio and the average savings ratio versus its relatively low-borrowing country, Argentina.

Note that all these examples, from the results in Tables 3–4, 3–5, and 3–6, are in disagreement with the research hypothesis as formulated in Chapter 1.

Table 3–5 clearly shows that the case of Korea versus Mexico is an exception in the sample. Even at a confidence level of more than 97.5 percent, and in most cases higher than 99 percent, Korea has been associated with more favorable values of growth indicators compared to Mexico. Again excluding Korea versus Mexico, Table 3–6 shows the indicators in three categories:

TABLE 3-6. Number of Indicators in Support of the Hypothesis versus Number of Indicators Not in Support of the Hypothesis

| Paired Countries | In Support Significantly Higher | Not in Support | | | Total Number of Indicators |
		Insignificantly Different	Significantly Lower*	Total	
Costa Rica Ecuador	3	4	1	5	8
Tunisia Paraguay	Ø	6	2	8	8
Panama Guatemala	Ø	5	3	8	8
Peru Portugal	2	3	3	6	8
Peru Colombia	2	6	Ø	6	8
Chile Argentina	2	2	2	4	6
Total	9	26	11	37	46

*We restated our previous test hypothesis in Table 3-4 as follows: Null hypothesis: average annual difference of a variable between a high-borrowing country and a low-borrowing country (the value for a high-borrowing country minus the value for a low-borrowing country) is equal to zero. Alternative hypothesis: average annual difference of a variable between a high-borrowing country and a low-borrowing country (the value for a high-borrowing country minus the value for a low-borrowing country) is less than zero.

Note: A confidence level of 95 percent has been used.

51

1. Number of indicators whose values have been significantly *higher* at a confidence level of 95 percent in favor of the high-borrowing country in each pair.
2. Number of indicators whose values have been *insignificant* at a confidence level of 95 percent between the high-borrowing country and the low-borrowing country in each pair.
3. Number of indicators whose values have been significantly *lower* (less favorable) at a confidence level of 95 percent for the high-borrowing country in each pair.

Additional striking results are seen through the categorization in Table 3–6. The total number of indicators whose average values are significantly lower (less favorable) for high-borrowing countries almost exceeds the total number of the indicators whose average values are significantly higher (more favorable) for the same countries. This contrast is well illustrated in Table 3–7, where the reader can see which indicator in which pair belongs to which category.

Note that only the first category of indicators (marked with "X") supports the research hypothesis. The number of these instances is only 9 of 46 tests. The purpose of Table 3–7 is to indicate that the pattern of the test results is far from confirming the research hypothesis. There is no variable in the cases of Tunisia versus Paraguay or Panama versus Guatemala to indicate that a high-borrowing country has performed, on the average, significantly better than its paired low-borrowing country. Conversely, the average values of the external gap and the internal gap in the case of Tunisia versus Paraguay and the average values of the incremental capital output ratio, the export/GDP ratio, and the external gap in the case of Panama versus Guatemala have been significantly less favorable on the part of the high-borrowing countries in the pairs. The average values of the marginal savings ratio, the average savings ratio, and the internal gap have been significantly lower (less favorable) for Peru, a major high-borrowing country, compared to Colombia. The same is true in the case of Chile, a high-borrowing country, versus Argentina with respect to the marginal savings ratio and the average savings ratio. Table 3–6 reveals 37 cases (tests) that are not in support of the hypothesis.

Considering such a high ratio of insignificant results (37/46) and having only nine instances of significantly higher values for the high-borrowing countries—even less than eleven instances of significantly less favorable values for the high-borrowing countries—the author cannot give a positive answer to the major question in the research.

TABLE 3-7. Pattern of Variables in Three Categories

Paired Countries	ICOR	Marginal Savings Ratio	Average Savings Ratio	Growth Rate of Export	Growth Rate of GDP	Export/ GDP	External Gap	Internal Gap
Costa Rica Ecuador	0	X	X	0	0	X	Z	0
Tunisia Paraguay	0	0	0	0	0	0	Z	Z
Panama Guatemala	Z	0	0	0	0	Z	Z	0
Peru Portugal	X	Z	Z	0	0	0	X	0
Peru Colombia	0	0	X	0	0	0	0	X
Chile Argentina	0	Z	Z	0	0	X	X	0

Notes: "X" indicates the first category: variables with significantly higher average values for the high-borrowing country. "0" indicates the second category: variables with insignificantly different values between the high-borrowing country versus the low-borrowing country. "Z" indicates the third category: variables with significantly lower average values for the high-borrowing country.

That is, the results do not confirm that between two countries with similar equity capital inflow but different levels of external borrowing, the country with a higher level of external borrowing has maintained more favorable growth indicators during the borrowing period under study. The statistical computations of a dichotomous test in Table 3–8 also show that the number of "positive" tests is not sufficient to support the research hypothesis. The very low F-ratio of .0509 in Table 3–8 indicates that the number of tests "in support" of the hypothesis is not statistically significant at a confidence level of even 75 percent.

In further verification of the results, two forms of regression analysis (regular and logarithmic) for individual high-borrowing countries in the sample were conducted. The formats of the regression equations are as follows:

$$Y = f \text{ (ICOR, MSR, } Xg, \text{ GDP}g)$$

$$\ln Y = f \text{ (ln ICOR, ln MSR, ln } Xg, \text{ ln GDP}g)$$

where

Y = annual external borrowing (deflated dollars)
ICOR = incremental capital output ratio
MSR = marginal savings ratio
Xg = growth rate of exports
GDPg = growth rate of GDP
ln = natural logarithm

The above variables were selected because each selected variable reflects a separate concept and tends to vary relatively independent of the others. Because these variables are derived values (ratios and percentages), one can be satisfied with their normal distribution, which is an assumption of regression analysis. A time lag of two years has been incorporated into the regression. The results of the first set of regressions (regular) and the results of the second set of regressions (logarithmic) are presented in Tables 3–9 and 3–10, respectively.

The results in both tables seem to be consistent with the previous tests. Korea, a major external borrower, is the exception, whose regression statistics are in agreement with the hypothesis. Table 3–9 shows a strong correlation (95 percent) between the deflated dollar values of external borrowing of Korea and its macroeconomic indicators. The F-ratio of the regression, indicative of a linear relationship between the dependent variable and all independent variables together, is 48.47. (The corresponding value in the

TABLE 3-8. Test of Dichotomous Data for the Variables in Table 3-5

Assumptions: "1" represents the variables whose values have been determined to be more favorable on the part of the high-borrowing country in a
pair. "0" represents the variables whose values have been determined not
to be more favorable on the part of the high-borrowing country in a pair.
(Table 3-5 is the basis for this dichotomy.)

Null hypothesis: The percentage of "1" is equal to the percentage of "0"
in the following table. Alternative hypothesis: The percentage of "1" is
different from the percentage of "0" in the table.

Number of Paired Countries	Variables								
	ICOR	Marginal Savings Ratio	Average Savings Ratio	Growth Rate of Export	Growth Rate of GDP	Export/GDP	External Gap: GDP	Internal Gap: GDP	Total
1	0	1	1	0	0	1	0	0	3
2	0	0	0	0	0	0	0	0	0
3	0	0	0	0	0	0	0	0	0
4	1	0	0	0	0	0	1	0	2
5	0	0	1	0	0	0	0	1	2
6	0	0	0	0	0	1	1	0	2
7	1	1	1	1	1	1	0	1	7
Total	2	2	3	1	1	3	2	2	16

$$\underline{G}^2 : \underline{kn} = 16^2 : 56 = 4.57 \qquad (1)$$

$$\underline{x}^2 = 16 \qquad (2)$$

$$\underline{T}_i{}^2 : \underline{n} = 36 : 7 = 5.14 \qquad (3)$$

$$\underline{P}_i{}^2 : \underline{k} = 70 : 8 = 8.75 \qquad (4)$$

55

TABLE 3-8. Continued

---

ssb pairs = (4) - (1) = 8.75 - 4.57 = 4.18

ssw pairs = (2) - (4) = 16 - 8.75 = 7.25

ss variables = (3) - (1) = 5.14 - 4.57 = .57

ss res = (2) - (3) - (4) + (1) = 16 - 5.14 - 8.75 + 4.57 = 6.68

ss total = (2) - (1) = 16 - 4.57 = 11.43

MS variable = ss variable : 7 DF = .57 : 7 = .081

MS res = ss res : 42 DF = 6.68 : 42 = .159

F-ratio = MS variable : MS res = .081 : .159 = .0509

Decision: Having an F-ratio of .0509, with 7 and 6 degrees of freedom, we cannot reject the null hypothesis.

Notation:

k = number of variables (treatments)

n = number of pairs (subjects)

x_i = the value of variable i for pair i

P_i = the sum of the k observation on pair i

T_i = the sum of the n observation on variable i

G = the grand mean of all observation

ssb pair = the between-pair variation

ssw pair = the within-pair variation

ss variables = the between-variable variation

ss res = the residual variation

MS = mean square

Note: For more information about dichotomous tests, see B. J. Winer, Statistical Principles in Experimental Design (New York: McGraw-Hill, 1971), pp. 303-05.

F-distribution table is 6.42 at a confidence level of 99 percent.) This means that the correlation (linear relationship) between the external debt and the macroindicators of Korea is significant at a confidence level of more than 99

TABLE 3-9. Level of External Debt versus Economic Indicators: Summary of Results of Multiple Regressions (1)

Regression	Borrowing LDC	R^2	F-Ratio of Regression & DF	Durbin-Watson	Coefficients and F-Ratio of Variables							
					ICOR	F	Marginal Savings Ratio	F	Growth Rate of Exports	F	Growth Rate of GDP	F
1	Costa Rica	.60	3.86 (4,10)	.90	-.04	.01	.84	9.39	.34	1.45	.18	.53
2	Tunisia	.20	.62 (4,10)	1.04	-.03	.008	-.002	.00	.44	2.23	-.04	.01
3	Panama	.48	2.40 (4,10)	.80	.55	4.28	.38	2.63	.42	2.59	-.23	.80
4	Peru	.63	3.19 (4,10)	1.73	-.59	3.86	-.19	.55	.14	.22	-.61	7.09
5	Chile	.03	.19 (2,10)	1.39	N/A	N/A	N/A		.09	.06	-.22	.38
6	Korea	.95	48.47 (4,10)	1.99	-.01	.04	-.12	2.94	-.87	6.12	1.81	26.68
6a	Korea	.82	26.68 (4,10)	1.99	.12	.96	-.01	.01	.91	50.08	*	

*Growth rate of GDP has been excluded because of its multicollinearity with growth rate of exports.

TABLE 3-10. Level of External Debt versus Economic Indicators: Summary of Results of Multiple Regression (11), Logarithmic Values

Regression	Borrowing LDC	R²	F-Ratio of Regression & DF	Durbin-Watson	ICOR	F	Marginal Savings Ratio	F	Growth Rate of Exports	F	Growth Rate of GDP	F
							Coefficients and F-Ratio of Variables					
7	Costa Rica	.67	5.20 (4,10)	1.00	-.49	4.36	.52	5.96	.19	.28	-.17	.22
8	Tunisia	.06	.17 (4,10)	1.42	-.06	.02	-.07	.03	-.17	.22	.19	.21
9	Panama	.34	1.30 (4,10)	.76	.41	1.92	.21	.58	.02	.01	-.44	2.82
10	Peru	.64	4.16 (4,10)	1.35	-.96	8.33	-.27	1.11	-.48	2.91	-.32	2.36
11	Chile	.24	1.59 (2,10)	2.50	N/A		N/A		-.04	.03	.49	3.15
12	Korea	.80	15.48 (4,10)	1.03	.28	4.46	.02	.03	.85	40.40	*	

*Growth rate of GDP has been excluded because of its multicollinearity with growth rate of export.

58

percent. The Durbin-Watson value, indicative of autocor-
relation, is also significant at a confidence level of more
than 99 percent. This was also verified by the plot residu-
als that the data do not have a serial correlation to violate
a required assumption of the regression. However, the
coefficients of individual variables in the case of Korea
(regression 6, Table 3-9) are unexpected. There are
negative signs for the coefficients of both the growth rate
of exports (-.87) and the marginal savings ratio (-.12).
These unexpected negative signs mainly stem from the
multicollinearity between the growth rates of exports and
the GDP in the case of Korea, as reflected in Table 3-11.
    There is a collinearity of .974 between the growth rate
of the GDP and the growth rate of exports, which has
influenced the signs of the variables in regression 6. In
an attempt to correct the situation, the growth rate of the
GDP was excluded, and a new multiple regression, with the
remaining three variables, was run. The result is regression 6a in Table 3-9. The coefficient of determination is
strong (.82) and the F-ratio of 26.68 is still significant at a
confidence level exceeding 99 percent. The sign for the
growth rate of export became positive (.91), with an F-
ratio of 50.08, which is also significant at a confidence level
of more than 99 percent. True, there is still a negative
sign for the marginal savings ratio. However, one must
notice that the coefficient (.01) is too weak to make a
strong interpretation about this negative sign. There is a
positive sign for the ICOR of Korea. But this positive
sign, with an F-ratio of .96, is statistically insignificant at
a confidence level of even 75 percent. Therefore the major
economic indicators to which the strong correlation could be

TABLE 3-11. Correlation Coefficient Matrix in the Case of Korea

	ICOR	MSR	Export Growth	GDP Growth	Debt
ICOR	1	.108	-.105	-.017	-.029
Marginal savings ratio		1	-.007	-.063	-.006
Export growth			1	.974	.896
GDP growth				1	.955

attributed are the growth rate of exports in regression 6a and the growth rate of the GDP in regression 6 for the case of Korea.

Unlike Korea, the correlation between the level of borrowing and the selected variables is weak for other countries in the sample. The coefficient of determination (R^2) for these countries ranges from .03 for Chile to a maximum of 63 percent for Peru. Taking a 95 percent level of confidence, the F-ratio of the regression for only Costa Rica is statistically significant. Yet the F-ratios for the coefficients of the ICOR, the growth rate of exports, and the growth rate of the GDP in the case of Costa Rica are all insignificant at the same level of confidence (see Table 3–9).

Because there has been no strong linear relationship between the level of borrowing and the values of the selected economic indicators, except for the case of Korea, a set of logarithmic regression was also executed (see Table 3–10). The case of Korea remains valid as before. The F-ratio of the new regression (15.48) is significant at a confidence level of more than 99 percent, and the coefficient of determination is still the highest (.80) in the sample. The poor correlation is still true for Tunisia, Panama, and Chile. The coefficients of determination for these countries are .06, .24, and .34, respectively. The corresponding values of the F-ratio of the regressions are also very low. The cases of Costa Rica and Peru have slightly improved as the new values of R^2 increased to .67 and .64, respectively, and the corresponding F-ratios are significant at a confidence level of 95 percent (see Table 3–9).

Yet note that the signs for the marginal savings ratio, the growth rate of exports, and the growth rate of the GDP for Peru are all negative. These negative signs could not have been traced back to the existence of a multicollinearity among the variables. Besides, the poor economic performance of Peru (discussed in Chapter 4) is in conformity with these negative coefficients. Strikingly, these negative coefficients are significant at a confidence level of 97.5 percent for the growth rate of exports and the growth rate of the GDP in the case of Peru. With respect to Costa Rica, the F-ratio of the logarithmic regression is 5.20, which is significant at a confidence level of more than 95 percent. However, this favorable result cannot be supported strongly because the Durbin-Watson is low, the coefficients of variables are insignificant for the growth rate of exports and the growth rate of the GDP at a confidence level of even 70 percent, and the coefficient of determination (.67) is not very impressive.

It is beyond the scope of this book to investigate the causes for a poor association between debt and economic growth of the individual countries. The explanation varies from one country to another. The results of regression analysis have already shown that there is a weak correlation between the level of borrowing and the values of economic indicators, at least in the cases of Panama, Tunisia, Peru, and Chile. Considering the results of the previously paired *t*-tests, Panama becomes even more intriguing. None of the average annual values of the economic indicators of Panama has been significantly more favorable than those of its paired low-borrowing country, Guatemala (see Table 3–5), whereas the average annual values of debt inflow to Panama increased throughout the period under study (see Table 3–2).

In view of these extreme results, an explanation regarding the striking disassociation of the external borrowing of Panama with the values of its economic growth indicators follows.

As a geographical fact, the economy of Panama is greatly influenced by the traffic and business activities in the Canal Zone. As Table 3–12 suggests, the transactions with the Canal Zone are crucial for the balance of payments of Panama. With regard to the exports of merchandise, about one-fifth of the total revenue is generated from the transactions with the Canal Zone, and about one-third of the travel income is from the Canal Zone. More than 90 percent of the labor income received by the Panamanians is a result of the employment opportunities in the canal. More than 70 percent of other goods and services in the balance of payments of Panama is generated from the trade with the Canal Zone.

In the light of this strong dependency, Table 3–13 was prepared to illustrate the trend of the contribution of the Canal Zone to the balance of payments of Panama in the 1970s. The table tends to suggest that the contribution of the zone has declined since 1974. More specifically, the ratio of the total revenue from the zone to the total import expenditures of Panama dropped form 46 percent in 1972 to 34 percent in 1976 and further declined to 28 percent in 1978.

The implications of these findings are that a declining contribution of the Canal Zone to the balance of payments of Panama partially explains the deterioration of the values of exports, GDP, and the trade deficit and their low associ-

TABLE 3-12. Transactions of Panama with Canal Zone (millions of SDRs)

	1972	1973	1974	1975	1976	1977	1978	1979
Export to merchandise	134.6	135.6	208.6	272.5	233.0	245.8	235.4	258.6
To Canal Zone	22.5	209	52.2	52.04	43.1	44.0	50.5	N/A
Portion of total	16%	15%	25%	19%	18%	17%	21%	N/A
To rest of world	112.1	114.7	220.1	220.1	189.9	201.8	184.9	N/A
Portion of total	84%	85%	75%	81%	82%	83%	79%	N/A
Travel income	80.4	89.8	104.7	112.8	133.8	152.1	162.5	179.7
With Canal Zone	36.0	32.7	33.5	32.7	34.4	36.4	42.7	N/A
Portion of total	44%	36%	31%	28%	25%	23%	26%	N/A
With rest of world	44.4	57.1	71.2	80.2	99.4	115.7	119.8	N/A
Portion of total	56%	64%	69%	72%	75%	77%	74%	N/A
Labor income	67.7	66.9	71.5	77.8	86.5	94.7	102.8	104.6
From Canal Zone	65.6	64.5	68.2	73.6	81.7	88.5	95.5	N/A
Portion of total	96%	96%	95%	94%	94%	93%	92%	N/A
From rest of world	2.1	2.4	3.3	4.2	4.8	6.2	6.9	N/A
Portion of total	4%	4%	5%	6%	6%	7%	8%	N/A
Other goods and services	71.7	75.9	93.5	95.6	119.5	153.4	148.1	206.0
To Canal Zone	50.3	54.4	66.1	67.4	85.0	105.4	134.9	N/A
Portion of total	70%	71%	70%	70%	71%	68%	91%	N/A
To rest of world	21.4	21.5	27.4	28.2	34.5	48.0	46.3	N/A
Portion of total	30%	29%	30%	30%	29%	32%	9%	N/A

Source: Calculations based on data from International Monetary Fund, Balance of Payments Yearbook (December 1980), vol. 31.

TABLE 3-13. Contribution by the Canal Zone to the Balance of Payments of Panama (millions of SDRs)

	1972	1973	1974	1975	1976	1977	1978	1979
Total revenue from Canal Zone to Panama								
Merchandise	22.5	20.9	52.2	52.4	43.1	44.0	50.5	N/A
Passenger service	3.6	7.2	11.4	11.7	13.4	14.0	14.2	14.6
Other transportation	48.6	46.2	120.2	113.1	108.2	99.8	69.4	72.4
Travel transactions	36.0	32.7	33.5	32.6	34.4	36.4	42.7	N/A
Foreign officials	8.2	9.4	10.7	13.2	13.3	13.7	13.5	20.7
Labor income	65.6	64.5	68.2	73.6	81.7	88.5	95.9	N/A
Other services	71.7	75.9	93.5	95.6	119.5	153.4	148.1	N/A
Total revenue	256.2	256.8	389.7	379.0	413.6	449.8	434.3	N/A
Total import expenditures (goods and services)	551.4	596.3	1,064.8	1,141.9	1,215.2	1,321.5	1,548.7	1,878.6
Total revenue from zone: total import expenditures	46%	43%	36%	33%	34%	34%	28%	N/A

Source: Calculations based on data from International Monetary Fund, Balance of Payments Yearbook (December 1980), vol. 31.

ation with the high levels of external borrowing in the 1970s.

Also, the export of bananas and refined petroleum, the major sources of export revenue, was not very favorable to Panama's balance of payments. The indexes for the export volume and the export prices in Table 3–13 reflect the fact that there has been no major improvement in the export revenue from the sale of bananas and particularly of refined petroleum since 1975. The volume of export drastically declined after 1975 for refined petroleum due to the rising cost of crude oil imported from Venezuela. And the volume of export of bananas has not increased impressively since 1975, partially because of periodic floods, bad weather, and competition from neighboring countries.[11] There has been no real improvement in the actual price of exported bananas from 1975 to 1979 (see Table 3–14).

The explanation for the deteriorating ICOR of Panama is not unrelated to what has been discussed so far. A plausible explanation for an increasing ICOR is that the GDP of Panama is directly affected by the revenue from Canal Zone–related activities. In view of a declining share of revenue from the zone, and a deteriorating export revenue from refined petroleum and bananas, the total value of GDP has been adversely affected. Therefore ICOR, which is directly a function of GDP, has increased (become more unfavorable) through the 1970s. In other words, an increasing rate of ICOR is another manifestation of a decreasing growth rate of GDP over time. Another probable explanation for an increasing ICOR is that the slack activities in the zone during the recession, coupled with the declining export of refined petroleum after 1975, created an excess capacity that subsequently led to a striking growth of ICOR in the economy.

Faced with rising trade and budget deficits in the 1970s, the government tapped internal and external financial outlets to finance the deficits.[12] (According to data in *International Financial Statistics,* the budget deficit had grown from $148 million in 1975 to $275 million in 1979.) The National Bank of Panama, which acts as the fiscal agent for the government, financed a major portion of the deficits. This is supported by the fact that the amount of the bank's claims on the government sector increased from less than $20 million in 1970 to around $250 million in 1979 (*International Financial Statistics*).

The Panamanian government also started to borrow more and more from external official and private international financial institutions throughout the 1970s. The data in Table 3–15 reflect the magnitude of the rising external debt

TABLE 3-14. Export Indexes of Panama (millions of SDRs)

	1972	1973	1974	1975	1976	1977	1978	1979
Volume of export	69	65	76	100	76	84	85	84
Bananas	114	112	90	100	100	109	119	110
Refined petroleum	53	41	68	100	48	46	44	35
Unit value of export	50	58	92	100	100	98	94	124
Bananas	95	96	93	100	104	103	101	100
Refined petroleum	32	46	99	100	109	116	108	103

Source: International Monetary Fund, International Financial Statistics.

TABLE 3-15. Loans to Panama

	1972	1973	1974	1975	1976	1977	1978
Official creditors							
Annual external loans							
(millions $U.S.)	15.8	70.5	36.8	127.4	72.0	243.4	73.0
Interest rate (%)	3.8	5.1	2.3	5.6	6.6	8.0	4.9
Maturity (years)	27.5	26.2	36.2	21.5	18.5	18.6	18.0
Private creditors							
Annual external loans							
(millions $U.S.)	90.1	211.5	114.1	280.2	250.4	251.1	933.1
Interest rate (%)	8.1	9.6	11.5	9.2	8.7	8.4	9.4
Maturity (years)	8.1	9.4	10.7	7.8	6.6	7.0	10.3
Total outstanding disbursed							
only (millions $U.S.)	345	457	564	774	1,110	1,354	1,905
Average terms of loans							
to the LDCs (private)							
Interest rate (%)	7.3	9.1	9.7	8.8	7.9	8.1	9.4
Maturity (years)	8.9	10.8	10.1	7.8	8.1	8.0	8.9

Source: World Bank, World Debt Tables.

66

of Panama since the early 1970s. For example, the share of private external loans had a spectacular tenfold increase from 1972 to 1978. Meantime, the total outstanding loans disbursed showed a remarkable increase from $345 million in 1972 to $1,905 million in 1978. In view of the fact that Panama was faced with rising deficits, deteriorating growth rates of export in both bananas and refined petroleum, and a declining share of revenue from the Canal Zone, one may logically infer that a good portion of the external loans has been used to pay the rising import bills and to balance the trade and budget deficits.

A higher interest rate charged to Panama by private lenders, compared to the average terms of loans for other LDCs, may also suggest that these loans were categorized by the lenders as balance of payment loans (see Table 3–15). However, neither public nor private international creditors hesitated to lend to Panama throughout the 1970s. Plausible reasons are the facts that Panama has the sovereignty of a waterway critical to the West and serves as the host of the Free Zone—the "Switzerland of the Western Hemisphere." Panama uses a strong currency like the U.S. dollar in its domestic and foreign transactions and has a stable government that is respected and supported by the international community.

As the outstanding external debt of Panama progressively mounted in the 1970s, a major portion of the new loans had to be allocated for the payment of the increasing debt services. This pressure was further compounded as the interest rate increased and the maturity of the new public debts dropped below 20 years and the maturity of the new private debt did not exceed a maximum of 10 years in the same period (see Table 3–15).

Table 3–16 gives the ratios of the debt service to the total loans disbursed. The data indicate that the debt service portion of the disbursed loans increased from 32 percent in 1969 to 69 percent in 1974 and 1975. In other words, in these two years only $31 from every $100 loan was the net monetary transfer on account of debt to the economy. Therefore the government had to borrow further to relieve temporarily the pressure of the debt service obligations. However, the ratio started to climb to 58 percent in 1978 and even further to 96 percent in 1979. The author tends to believe that the increasing debt service portion of the total debts is a partial explanation for the poor correlation between the level of external borrowing and the values of the economic indicators.

Meantime, the National Bank of Panama, as the only fiscal agent of the government, has proportionally shifted

TABLE 3-16. Debt Services of Panama (thousands $U.S.)

Year	Total Debt Disbursed (I)	Total Debt Services Paid (II)	Debt Service: Debt Disbursed (II:I)
1969	39,926	13,035	32%
1970	67,446	30,481	45%
1971	78,885	40,350	51%
1972	135,485	52,016	38%
1973	163,281	87,024	53%
1974	194,936	135,557	69%
1975	249,048	172,370	69%
1976	373,304	100,827	27%
1977	343,054	166,123	48%
1978	987,553	572,478	57%
1979	406,930	393,727	96%

Source: World Bank, World Debt Tables.

more of its resources, including the external debt, to the government sector. The calculations in Table 3–17 support this observation. The aggregated data indicate that while the portion of the bank's resources allocated to the private sector was 38 percent in 1974 (more than double that of the portion for the government sector), the pattern reversed over time. In 1979 the portion of the resources allocated to the private sector (29 percent) was much less than that of the government sector (33 percent). In 1976 almost half of the resources was allocated to the government consumption. These percentages illustrate that the National Bank of Panama has become more and more the banker of the government rather than of the private sector. This is consistent with the statistics indicating that the government has faced increasing trade and budget deficits since the early 1970s.

CONCLUSION

The results of the empirical analysis show no systematic relationship between foreign loans and economic indicators. In explaining the case of Panama, a declining portion of revenue from the Canal Zone, a deteriorating export mar-

TABLE 3-17.   National Bank of Panama

	1974	1975	1976	1977	1978	1979
Claims on government (millions $U.S.)	62.2 (18%)	98.0 (25%)	194.1 (49%)	167.7 (36%)	163.4 (27%)	248.9 (33%)
Claims on private sector (millions $U.S.)	130.4 (38%)	140.7 (36%)	124.4 (31%)	121.8 (26%)	175.5 (29%)	216.3 (29%)
Major sources (time and savings deposit plus capital accounts) (millions $U.S.)	341.5	381.8	390.3	458.0	586.5	745.0

Source: International Monetary Fund, International Financial Statistics, September 1981.

ket, a rising debt service portion of the total external loans, and rising trade and budget deficits—all interrelatedly explain the extreme disassociation of the aggressive borrowing of Panama with the values of its economic indicators.

The interpretations for the case of Panama are consistent with a final conclusion that a high level of external borrowing per se is not a sufficient condition for higher values of growth indicators. This view at least can be generalized to the cases of the borrowing LDCs for which the paired t-tests and multiple regressions were executed. This conclusion is not inconsistent with the views of some scholars such as Gerald M. Meier and A. K. Cairncross. Meier points out that the major theories supporting the external capital as the dominant input of growth make a "mutatis mutandis" assumption, that is, all other factors that must cooperate with capital do cooperate when capital increases. This may be a reasonable assumption for an advanced economy, but not necessarily for a capital-importing LDC, Meier argues.[13]

Although Cairncross believes that growth and the volume of capital are "closely interrelated" and that the major theories of economic development are built on this interaction, he questions whether more capital per se will bring more acceleration in production.[14] In a hypothetical case, where an additional investment yields a zero return on investment, an infinite volume of increment capital provides a zero contribution to the national income. This example raises the issue of the purpose and uses of borrowing. Leaving the latter factor aside, the results of the statistical analysis indicate that the level of external loans on the part of the LDCs is not a strong explanatory factor for the values of their growth indicators.

In further clarification of the results, a related supplementary question has been formulated: What has been the motivation (purpose and uses) of the external borrowing? A thorough investigation of this question requires a case study for each country in the sample. Considering the scope of this book, the author has selected two opposing cases—Korea and Peru. The results of the empirical analysis show that Korea has been the exceptional case in the sample. Peru, another major borrowing country, represents an opposite case whose size of economy is relatively closest to that of Korea. These two case studies are presented in Chapter 4 to examine the motivation of borrowing as a possible explanation for association/disassociation of the level of external borrowing with the values of growth indicators.

NOTES

1. Jasbir Chopra et al., "U.S. Foreign Divestment: A 1972–1975 Updating," *Colombia Journal of World Business* 13 (1976): 14–18.
2. Ibid. For more information about disinvestment, see J. J. Boddewyn, *International Divestments: A Survey of Corporate Experience* (Geneva and New York: Business International), chap. 2.
3. World Bank, *Chile: An Economy in Transition* (January 1980), pp. 102–8.
4. Ibid.
5. Ibid.
6. World Bank, *Portugal, Current and Prospective Economic Trends* (November 1978), p. 39.
7. Ibid., pp. 1–3.
8. Rosemary Thorp et al., *Peru 1890–1977, Growth and Policy in an Open Economy* (New York: Columbia University Press, 1978), p. 301.
9. Carlos Pagano, *External Financing Prospects of Latin America's Development Banking System* (Inter-American Development Bank, 1979), pp. 17–18.
10. U.S. Treasury, *International Finance,* annual report

to the president and to Congress for 1978, p. 35.

11.   Robert E. Looney, *The Economic Development of Panama* (New York: Praeger, 1976).

12.   Robert Looney reports that since the early 1970s, the government of Panama used even the social security system of the country to finance its rising deficits.   Domestic suppliers and contractors were also expected to accept government bonds rather than hard cash.   This has been an informal condition for a contractor if he wanted to be on the regular list of the government contractors.   See Robert E. Looney, *The Economic Development of Panama* (New York: Praeger, 1976), pp. 127–31.

13.   See Gerald M. Meier, "Criticism of Capital-Output Ratio-Note," *Leading Issues in Economic Development* (New York: Oxford University Press, 1976), p. 259.

14.   A. K. Cairncross, "The Place of Capital in Economics," in Meier, *Leading Issues in Economic Development,* p. 264.

4

Case Analysis

THE CASE OF KOREA

From the liberation of Korea from Japan in 1945 until a military coup in May 1961, the Korean economy suffered from a series of events that impeded that country from pursuing any political and economic direction. The absence of a firm political leadership created a chaotic domestic situation, which was detrimental to economic development, throughout the periods of the American military government (1945–48), the inward-looking and unstable regime of Syngman Rhee (1948–60), the tragic Korean War (1950–53), the Student Revolution (April 1960), the organized regime of Chang Mayon (1960–61), and finally a military coup (May 1961).[1] It is from October 1963, when the third republic was established and Park Chung Hee became president of a civilian government, that Korea entered a stable era for economic development.

In Chapter 3 it was concluded that the economic performance of Korea has been exceptionally associated with a high level of external borrowing since 1963. This is also consistent with a comparative report by the United Nations that Korea was an exception, with an annual growth rate exceeding its planned rate, from the mid-1960s to the early 1970s, among a sample of 30 LDCs.[2] In reference to this phenomenal growth in the last two decades, Wade and Kim commented that "Korean development is no miracle, but some measure of its mystery will remain to intrigue future scholars."[3] Larry Westphal suggested that the answer can be found in the political changes in the early 1960s that brought to power a leadership committed to economic development and effective policies.[4] Recently, Leroy Jones and Il Sakong stressed the interaction of the government and the business community as a major factor for the Korean growth: "The Korean miracle is not a triumph of laissez-faire, but of a pragmatic non-ideological mixture of market and non-market forces," they argue.[5]

It is not the purpose of this book to identify the various factors that contributed to Korea's phenomenal growth.[6] Focusing on the issue of external borrowing, the objectives here are to explain the rising inflow of debt to Korea and to examine the motivation (purpose and uses) of borrowing as a possible explanation for the strong association of Korean debt with its economic performance.

In this investigation, it has been assumed that the motivation of borrowing is reflected in the major government policies that have affected the inflow of external debt and the pattern of spending (allocation) of external borrowing in the economy. (Consistently, the same assumptions hold true in the analysis of the case of Peru.) Throughout this analysis, the author's assessment of the related facts and figures will be verified by the views and the knowledge of the experts in the subject.

INCREASING INFLOW OF EXTERNAL DEBT INTO KOREA

From the beginning, the government of President Park adopted major policies and revised some of the old policies to import foreign capital to finance the increasing shortage of investment expenditures. The new government admitted the fact that foreign aid was no longer a reliable and sufficient source for Korea's external financing. The total aid received by Korea in 1964, the second year of the civilian government, substantially declined. The ratio of aid to the import expenditures declined from 83.6 percent in 1960 to 41.8 percent in 1963 and decreased further to 32.2 percent in 1965.[7]

In response to the chronic shortage of foreign currencies, the government adopted a multifaceted policy to attract new foreign capital. Economic missions were sent to the United States and the industrialized European countries to encourage both governments and private institutions to participate in financing the selected projects of the first five-year plan. Expeditious procedures were developed by the Foreign Capital Inducement Deliberation Committee to facilitate the export credits for the purchase of capital goods from the industrialized countries. In an attempt to reduce the bureaucracy, the committee became the sole authority to process applications for foreign loans and to approve or reject the proposed projects.

The government also decided to guarantee approved foreign loans, making the government legally responsible to reschedule or honor the obligations of a debtor in the case of a possible default. A new Foreign Capital Inducement Law, revised in 1966, made it clear that the government was authorized to supervise the management and property of any foreign-financed firm that became insolvent.[8] In order to make the new guarantee policy more accountable, the government made a prudent requirement that the annual debt service of the guaranteed loans should not exceed 9 percent of their total annual disbursements. A series of tax concessions was also granted to stimulate the inflow of funds, including the exemption of the interest income of the approved foreign loans from a 40 percent corporation income tax.

The interest rate reform of October 1965 was another major policy deliberately enacted by the government to stimulate foreign borrowing.* Before this reform, the commercial bank rates on deposits and loans were significantly lower than those offered in the curb market. Through this reform, the ceilings on both deposit rates and lending rates were raised significantly. The interest rate on borrowing from domestic sources increased to 26 percent and the rate on domestic loans for the selected projects rose to 18 percent.[9] As a result, foreign loans, compared to domestic loans, became very attractive. The interest rate on foreign loans with the government guarantee became even more favorable in the market.

There was another reason why foreign borrowing became more attractive to the borrowers. Considering the facts that the exchange rate in Korea was pegged at 271 won to the U.S. dollar from 1965 to 1967, and the won was not significantly devaluated until mid-1971, the effective interest rate (real cost) on a foreign currency denominated loan was even lower than the concessionary nominal rates set by the government. This point is supported by the calculations of Frank, Wade and Kim, and Westphal, showing that the effective interest rates on foreign loans were always

---

*Another major reason for this reform was to generate more domestic savings by encouraging people to rechannel their disposable funds from hoarding or further consumption into banks' savings deposits.

negative during the period of 1965–1970. In contrast, the calculations of Wontack Hong show that in the same period the effective interest rates on domestic loans were always positive.[10] This means that foreign borrowing, in the absence of a sufficient devaluation of the won, became a source of economic gain for the borrowers after the interest rate reform of October 1965. Therefore the reform served as an incentive policy to stimulate the flow of foreign debt into the economy.

In view of such favorable conditions, the inflow of foreign debt sharply increased in the mid-1960s. The data in Table 4–1 suggest that 1966 was the starting point for the rise of foreign debt in Korea. Note that 64 percent of the total disbursed loans in 1966 were granted by the private lenders. This implies that the new government succeeded in presenting Korea in the financial markets, from even the beginning, as a creditworthy borrowing LDC. Private loans phenomenally increased from $110.3 million in 1966 to $407.9 million in 1968, equal to an annual increase of 90 percent. Throughout 1966–70, official loans were also increasing, mainly in the form of bilateral loans, while the portion of the multilateral loans remained at a very low level.

From 1969 to 1972, the inflow of private debt into Korea did not grow and even declined by 28 percent in 1970 (see Table 4–1). There are two explanations for this stagnant/declining period of private debt inflow. First, all external loans were denominated in the U.S. dollar or other foreign currencies. There was a gradual devaluation of the won from the beginning of 1968 until June 1971, when the won was sharply devaluated to 370 won per U.S. dollar. This devaluation eroded the economic gain of external borrowing, which was in the form of a negative interest rate, as previously noted. There was some speculation by prospective borrowers that the devaluation of the won would be tactical and temporary. Therefore some businesspeople preferred to postpone their borrowing until revaluation occurred and reversed the situation to that of the mid-1960s. Consistent with this interpretation is a report that demand for borrowing subsided by the devaluation of June 1971 and by the rapidly sliding peg in early 1972.[11]

The other explanation for the stagnant private borrowing is the rise of the debt service ratio in the early 1970s, which created some concern about the ability of the Korean economy to pay its rising debts. The debt service ratio of Korea exceeded 30 percent in 1970, which was unusually high for a borrowing LDC. Purposely, but temporarily, the government put some ceilings on new private borrowing and, meantime, managed to reorganize some of the outstanding loans. It is in this period, as reflected in Table 4–1, that the volume of the official loans relatively increased to relieve the debt service pressure of the early 1970s.

Table 4–1 suggests, however, that the stagnant period for private debt inflow did not last very long. Private borrowing started to rise again in 1973, with a growth rate of 40 percent over the previous year. Businesspeople apparently became convinced that the sharp devaluation of 1971 would not reverse and that the won would continue to reflect a more realistic parity versus foreign currencies in the market.

Another important observation in Table 4–1 is that private borrowing has outpaced official borrowing since 1973. The annual rates of growth in private borrowing were 40, 42, 45, -6, 48, and 105 percent in 1973 to 1978, respectively. The corresponding rates for official borrowing were 29, -23, 26, 33, -5, and 16 percent. Although the growth rate of private borrowing declined to 16 percent in 1979, its portion of the total disbursed loans still remained as high as 78 percent in the same year.

In interpreting this rising trend, it should be pointed out that the major portion of official loans to Korea, until the mid-1970s, was bilaterally financed by the U.S. government through concessional terms. As the policy of the U.S. government shifted toward an international involvement for multilateral loans, the American bilateral source of financing lost its significance. This statement is supported by the data in Table 4–2, where the monetary values of the total aid and government loans, from the United States to Korea, remained relatively stationary throughout the period of 1966 to 1975, except in 1972. The total value of American aid and government loans to Korea was as low as $81.7 million in 1974. In view of a declining share of official loans in general, and the U.S. bilateral loans in particular, in the mid-1970s Korean policymakers had no option other than to shift to the private international capital markets.

Meantime the private markets were glutted with the ready-to-be-recycled petrodollars. Korea, with a good history of borrowing and an excellent performance of exports, was at the top of the list of the creditworthy borrowers. It is at this juncture that Korea, faced with rising investment expenditures, decided to make a relative shift from "soft" loans to "hard" loans. This shift was in fact a mechanism to adjust the Korean economy to the new shock of the quadrupling prices of imported oil. The latter event raised the import expenditures of Korea beyond its export revenues and created a widening external gap (trade

TABLE 4-1. External Debt Inflow to Korea (millions of U.S. dollars)

	1963	1964	1965	1966	1967	1968	1969	1970	1971
Total Disbursements		18.7	44.2	172.4	196.7	479.6	588.7	440.4	715.9
Official loans			44.2	62.1	82.1	71.7	186.9	153.7	304.6
(Portion of total disbursements)				36%	41%	14%	31%	34%	42%
Multilateral				0	0	8.3	10.5	13.1	59.3
Bilateral				62.1	82.1	63.4	176.3	140.6	245.2
Private loans			*	110.3	114.6	407.9	401.8	286.7	411.3
(Portion of total disbursements)				64%	59%	86%	69%	66%	58%
Suppliers									258.3
Financial markets									153.0
Annual growth rates									
Official loans					32%	-12%	160%	-17%	98%
Private loans					3%	255%	-1%	-28%	43%

	1972	1973	1974	1975	1976	1977	1978	1979
Total Disbursements	811.7	1,090.6	1,180.5	1,634.6	1,775.7	2,213.4	3,916.6	4,647.9
Official loans	437.8	565.5	434.9	551.4	738.5	700.7	812.8	1,050.3
(Portion of total disbursements)	53%	51%	36%	33%	41%	31%	20%	22%
Multilateral	71.9	99.7	150.3	291.8	380.8	285.4	413.1	517.1
Bilateral	365.8	465.8	284.5	259.5	357.6	415.3	399.6	533.2
Private loans	374.9	525.0	745.6	1,083.2	1,017.2	1,512.6	3,103.7	3,597.6
(Portion of total disbursements)	47%	49%	64%	67%	59%	69%	80%	78%
Suppliers	230.1	317.5	336.6	560.1	457.1	682.2	1,668.0	699.2
Financial markets	144.8	207.5	408.5	523.1	560.0	830.4	1,435.7	2,898.3
Annual growth rates								
Official loans	43%	29%	-23%	26%	33%	-5%	16%	29%
Private loans	-81%	40%	42%	45%	-6%	48%	105%	16%

Note: The sum of loans in some categories may not exactly equal the total due to rounding.
*Negligible.
Source: World Bank, World Debt Tables.

TABLE 4-2. Total Aid and Government Loans from the United States to Korea, 1966-75 (millions of U.S. dollars)

Year	Total Aid	Other U.S. Government Loans	Total
1966	173.2	64.4	237.6
1967	229.8	64.0	293.8
1968	197.5	79.5	277.0
1969	239.7	61.4	301.1
1970	181.8	55.1	236.9
1971	185.9	124.4	310.3
1972	241.4	275.4	516.8
1973	92.1	188.4	280.5
1974	46.2	35.0	81.7
1975	277.0	102.8	379.8

Source: USAID, Korea.

deficit) in subsequent years. The external gap increased phenomenally from about 404 billion won in 1973 to around 971 billion in 1974.[12] Therefore aggressive borrowing from the private markets and, consequently, the emergence of a rising trend in the private loans were natural responses to an increasing need for new and reliable financial sources.

The following section examines where those imported loans have basically been invested.

A LOOK INTO THE MOTIVATION
OF EXTERNAL BORROWING

As stated previously, the motivation (purpose and uses) of borrowing is reflected in the major policies and reforms that are periodically enacted by the government of a borrowing country. The sectorial distribution of foreign loans and the priorities for domestic investments are the relevant factors for understanding what objective(s) an aggressively borrowing country pursues in its borrowing policy.

Government economic planning in Korea is the responsibility of the Economic Planning Board (EPB), which has considerable formal power and political support to develop comprehensive five-year economic plans for the country. The EPB, through consultation with the Korean Development

Institute (KDI) and foreign experts, initiates the general guidelines for economic planning and the sectorial allocation of available resources. These general guidelines are sent to all executive units (ministries and their divisions) in the government to define their own activities and develop the specific proposals. The executive units, in consultation with and cooperation from the public and private enterprises concerned, prepare and submit their proposals to the EPB. The EPB makes the necessary modifications and forwards the proposed plans to the Cabinet Planning Committee and Advisory Committee, which operate under the prime minister. For a further review and additional refinement, the proposed package of planning is also evaluated by the Economic-Science Council (ESC) before it is presented to the Cabinet Council. Following the approval of the Cabinet Council, the package is submitted to the president for final endorsement.[13]

In the first five-year economic plan (1962–66), the government emphasized three key factors: manufacturing, energy, and social overhead capital. The share of manufacturing of the total budget was 34 percent and that of power, transportation, and communication was about 50 percent.[14] As stated in the plan, the success of the Korean economy would depend on its industrialization. During the plan period, emphasis was placed on the development of power, coal, and other energy sources, improvement of the balance of international payments through increased exports, and advanced technology.[15] This implies that the objective of the new government, from even the early years of military rule, was to build a base for industrialization. The sectorial distribution of foreign loans in the first five-year plan reflects the government's commitment to an industrialization-based growth (see Table 4–3).

Table 4–3 indicates that of a total of $426 million in foreign loans, about $227.8 million (53 percent) was allocated to the secondary sector, mainly manufacturing, in the plan period of 1962–66. Of $683.6 million available in foreign exchange, about $365.2 (53 percent) was allocated to the manufacturing sector. Note that the share of foreign loans ($426 million) constituted about 62 percent of the total foreign exchange requirements ($683.6 million). Thus the interpretation is that foreign loans were the main source of the foreign exchange requirements in this period, and foreign loans were used mainly in the manufacturing sector.

The second five-year plan (1967–71) was an extension of the previous plan to strengthen the industrial base of Korea. With the help of domestic as well as foreign exports, the old guidelines were revised to focus on the

TABLE 4-3. Foreign Exchange Allocation, Plan Period 1962-66 (millions of U.S.dollars)

	Primary Industry	Secondary Industry	Tertiary Industry	Total
Foreign loans	14.9	227.8	183.3	426.0
Korean foreign exchange	10.5	137.4	78.1	226.0
International Cooperation Administration	--	--	22.7	22.7
AID	--	--	8.9	8.9
Total	25.4	365.2	293.0	683.6

Source: Republic of Korea, Summary of the First Five-Year Economic Plan (1962-66), (Seoul, 1962), p. 72, Table 10.

manufacturing sector and particularly on the export indus-tries. According to statistics published by the Economic Planning Board of Korea, of a total of $1,388 million avail-able in foreign currency during the second five-year plan, about $709 million (51 percent) was allocated to the manu-facturing sector, with the objective of strengthening the base of the export industries.[16]

Irma Adelman, who was a consultant to the government of Korea and was active in the entire process of developing the second five-year plan, reports that the planning pro-cess included a thorough review of the South Korean econ-omy. A number of required reforms preceded the success-ful implementation of the economic plans in Korea.[17] The number and variety of these policy reforms, which were mostly directed toward the expansion of the export indus-tries, reflect the extent of how serious the government has been about its motivation for and commitment to an "ex-port-led growth" since the mid-1960s. Table 4-4 provides a chronology of the major policies of export promotion enacted since the early 1960s. Most of the export incentives in Table 4-4 are self-explanatory. However, further explana-tion of some of the policies help illustrate the significance of these reforms.

During much of the 1960s, there was a credit crunch for the businessperson in Korea. Various credit subsidies were put into effect to respond to this problem. For instance,

TABLE 4-4. Chronology of Major Export Incentive Policies Since the Military Government in May 1961

Sequential No.	Date Started	Date Expired	Incentive Policy
1	September 1961	--	Creation of exporters' association for various export products
2	October 1961	--	Financing imports of materials to be used in export products
3	September 1962	--	Financing suppliers of U.S. offshore military procurement
4	November 1962	--	Export-import link system
5	1964	--	Financing KOTRA
6	February 1964	--	Fund to convert small and medium-sized firms into export industries
7	March 1964	December 1973	Tariff exemptions on capital equipment for export production
8	July 1964	September 1969	Fund to promote the export industry
9	July 1965	--	Wastage allowance
10	1965	--	Discount on electricity rates
11	1965	--	Waiver issuance for shipping
12	February 1967	--	Differential treatment of traders based on export performance
13	May 1967	--	Foreign currency loans
14	January 1969	--	Export insurance
15	August 1969	--	Tax credit for foreign market development expenditures
16	October 1969	--	Financing exports on credit

TABLE 4-4. Continued

Sequential No.	Date Started	Date Expired	Incentive Policy
17	March 1973	--	Tax credit for losses due to operations in foreign markets
18	January 1974	--	Tariff payments on an installment basis for capital equipment used in export production
19	May 1975	--	General trading company
20	June 1976	--	Export-import bank

Source: Based on a list in Wontack Hong, "Trade, Distortion and Employment Growth in Korea," mimeograph (Seoul: Korea Development Institute Press, 1977), pp. 82-83. For a more detailed list, see also Jones and Sakong, Government, Business, and Entrepreneurship, pp. 94-95.

through two separate export funds—items 6 and 8 in Table 4-4—a maximum of 20 million won was granted as preferential loans to a single exporter at a modest interest rate. Various other export credits—items 2, 3, 13, 16, and 17—were available at highly preferential interest rates ranging from 3 to 6.5 percent. The credit was about 200 won per dollar to a single exporter upon the submission of a letter of credit.[18] Wastage allowance—item 9—generally exceeded in practice the actual amount of defective raw materials or goods imported for the export production. Therefore the result was an additional profit for the importers of the goods to be used for exports. In 1964, the government authorized the newly established Korean Trade Promotion Corporation (KOTRA) to collect 1 percent of the value of import proceeds as a financial base for the export promotion activities of KOTRA—item 5. KOTRA has been very active in international marketing for Korean export commodities in both developed and developing countries.

Table 4-4 is by no means exhaustive of the export promotion policies of the Korean government. However, it indicates that 1962-69 (particularly 1964 and 1965) was the time when the Korean government put its motivation (growth through export) aggressively into action. It is very important to note that the intensity of export promotion in this period (1964–65) was concurrent with the start of aggressive Korean borrowing in international capital markets, as discussed in the previous section.

Considering the concurrent events of rising foreign borrowing on the one hand and increasing export incentives on the other, the author logically infers that the motivation behind the aggressive foreign borrowing of Korea was to finance the export industries. In support of this interpretation, some data have been collected in Table 4–5 to identify the sectors in which foreign loans have been invested. Table 4–5 also provides the pattern of how foreign commercial and official loans were allocated among three sectors: the primary sector, the manufacturing sector, and the social overhead capital and service sector (SOCS). The data also reflect the allocation of foreign loans to the major industries within the manufacturing and SOCS sectors.

Table 4–5 indicates that in the period of 1967 to 1971 about 60 percent of the total commercial loans were used in the manufacturing sector and increased to about 66 percent in the period of 1972–75. Within the manufacturing sector, the shares of textiles, chemicals, petroleum, metals, and nonmetals were significant. The manufacturing sector was not excluded even in the sectorial distribution of official loans. About one-fifth of official loans was placed in the manufacturing sector, where the shares of chemicals and metals were considerable. A small portion of the commercial loans was allocated to the primary sector, which is mainly agricultural.

Note that although more than 60 percent of the total foreign commercial loans were allocated to the manufacturing sector in 1967–75, the government did not ignore the social and infrastructure areas. About 31 percent of the commercial loans were spent in social overhead capital and services. Electricity (55 percent) and transportation (38 percent) were the main concerns in the SOCS sector. However, the share of the SOCS of the total commercial loans declined in 1971–75 compared to the previous period.

In contrast to the sectorial allocation of commercial loans, the uses of official loans have been basically infrastructural. About three-quarters of the imported official loans have been channeled to the SOCS, mainly for electricity and transportation. Because transportation and electricity are the backbone of the manufacturing sector, the uses of official loans in the SOCS sector were, in fact, support, investments for the manufacturing sector. The share of the primary sector of the official loans was minimal and slightly higher than that of the commercial loans.

TABLE 4-5. Uses of Foreign Loans in Different Sectors of the Korean Economy (hundred thousands of U.S. dollars)

	Private Loans		Official Loans	
	1967-71	1972-75	1967-71	1972-75
Primary sector	195.2	194.8	71.0	242.8
Portion of primary sector of all sectors	5%	3%	5%	7%
Manufacturing sector	2,368.5	5,106.9	272.3	663.7
Portion of manufacturing sector of all sectors	60%	66%	19%	18%
Portion of major industries of total manufacturing				
Textiles	20%	14%	11%	3%
Chemicals	21%	24%	68%	45%
Petroleum	21%	16%	--	--
Metals and nonmetals	26%	25%	15%	42%
Other	8%	17%	4%	9%
Social overhead capital and service (SOCS)	1,367.3	2,462.0	1,055.1	2,779.7
Portion of SOCS of all sectors	35%	31%	76%	75%
Portion of major industries of all SOCS				
Electricity	51%	55%	26%	19%
Transportation	40%	38%	50%	51%
Others	9%	7%	24%	30%
All others	3,931.0	7,762.7	1,398.4	3,686.2

Source: Based on data from Wontack Hong, "Trade, Distortions and Employment Growth in Korea," mimeograph (Seoul: Korea Development Institute Press 1977).

Note: Sum of percentages may not equal 100 because of rounding.

Despite the fact that the data in Table 4–4 are partial, in terms of magnitude as well as timing, they serve as a base to indicate that the purpose of at least commercial foreign loans has been consistently to promote the manufacturing sector for the expansion of the export industries. This interpretation is also confirmed by some related statistics published by the Korean Economic Planning Board.

Table 4–6 indicates that the portion of capital goods and raw materials, imported for export production, has continuously increased since 1963. This simply means that available foreign exchange was increasingly used for the export industries. While the ratio of capital goods and raw materials imported for the export production was only 20.6 percent in 1963, it increased to 49.2 percent in 1970 and grew further to 58.2 percent in 1977.

The motivation of the Korean government for external loans as a source of capital can also be evaluated in a nonstatistical context. As Kwang Suk Kim argues, a growth strategy based on merely "import substitution" did not succeed in the years before the Park government because of a small domestic market and a lack of capital.[19] The poor natural resources of Korea was another deterrent to a growth strategy based on domestic resource utilization. Learning from the failure of past experience, Park's government made a substantial shift from the previous "import substitution" policy to an "export-led growth" strategy. In view of declining U.S. aid, which previously financed most of the import expenditures, the new government shifted to foreign loans as its main source of foreign capital to implement its growth strategy. The intensity of the government's motivation for growth is reflected in various measures, from imposing sanctions and setting export targets to generous export subsidies. The Ministry of Commerce and Industry, through its "export situation room," became responsible for monitoring the actual export performance against the targeted volumes of exports.[20]

Most of the export incentives established in the 1960s have remained in effect throughout the 1970s. And the government responded immediately with new policies to overcome any new bottlenecks that emerged in the process of export growth. For example, in 1970–72, a number of Korean exporters were faced with cash flow problems that brought a temporary slowdown in the growth of export production. Part of the reason for the cash flow problem was the rise of the foreign debt services of the exporters, due to the devaluation of the won to 400 per U.S. dollar by June 1972 and the accumulation of foreign loans of the exporters from the previous years. The government imme-

TABLE 4-6. Import Expenditure for Capital Goods and Raw Materials for Export Production (percentage of total import expenditures)

Year	Percentage	Year	Percentage
1961	13.4	1970	49.2
----	----	1971	49.7
1963	20.6	1972	57.5
1964	18.9	1973	64.1
1965	15.1	1974	56.8
1966	38.1	1975	56.3
1967	44.7	1976	55.1
1968	51.0	1977	58.2
1969	48.8		

Source: Economic Planning Board, Major Statistics of Korean Economy (Seoul, 1978).

diately reacted by an Emergency Act. Through this act, the outstanding loans were rescheduled. The government also announced that the new parity of the won versus the U.S. dollar and other currencies would remain stable. Consequently, the export production did improve.

As reported in Table 4–7, the average annual growth rate of exports in 1970–74 was about 42 percent, even slightly higher than the growth rate of 40 percent in 1965–69. True, the average annual rate of growth in exports in 1975–79 declined to 26 percent. However, such a lower rate should not be interpreted as a reverse commitment or a less serious motivation on the part of the government toward the expansion of exports in the latter part of the 1970s. The increasing prices of oil to which the cost of Korean export production is very sensitive, a slackening world market, and a rising competition from both the developed and developing countries are plausible explanations for the lower export performance in 1975–79. Furthermore, the annual export/GDP ratio noticeably improved from 17 percent in 1970–74 to 26 percent in 1975–79 (see Table 4–7).

Table 4–7 tends to indicate that the values of the ICOR, the marginal savings ratio, and the growth rate of the GDP, except for slight changes, remained steady throughout the period. This systematic growth is reflected particularly in the annual GDP growth rate of 9.7 percent in

TABLE 4-7. Korea: Periodic Average Values of Growth Indicators

Variables	1965-69	1970-74	1975-79
Incremental capital output ratio	.55	.70	.57
Marginal savings ratio	.236	.221	.209
Average savings ratio	.113	.217	.207
Growth rate of export	.408	.426	.261
Growth rate of GDP	.097	.096	.100
Export/GDP	.073	.178	.265
Internal gap	-.101	-.012	-.061
External gap	-.123	-.113	-.059

Source: International Monetary Fund, International Financial Statistics.
See Table 1-2 for the calculation procedure.

1965–69, 9.6 percent in 1970–74, and 10 percent in 1975–79. With respect to the export/GDP ratio and the external gap, the Korean performance continuously improved: 9.3, 17.8, and 26.5 percent in 1965–69, 1970–74, and 1975–79, respectively. As a consequence of export incentives and rising exports, Korea managed to reduce the annual external gap, as a portion of the GDP, from 12.3 percent in the period 1965–69, to 11.3 percent in 1970–74, and still further to 5.9 percent in 1975–79.

A strong motivation for an export-led growth throughout the 1970s is well reflected in the guidelines of the third (1972–76) and fourth (1977–81) five-year economic plans. According to Hak-Yul Kim, minister of the Economic Planning Board at the time of the third plan, the main emphasis of the third plan was, among other things, on improving the international balance of payments through rapid increase in exports and broadening the industrial base through the development of heavy and chemical industries.[21] (Table 4-4 shows that about 66 percent of the total foreign commercial loans of Korea were allocated to the manufacturing sector during that period.) The fourth five-year economic plan also stated that "We—Korea—must continue to expand exports, and at the same time, attempt to minimize our dependence on the international economy. To achieve these tasks, Korea must continue to improve the quality of its export commodities and diversify its markets."[22]

THE CASE OF PERU

Unlike Korea, the economic and political directions in Peru were unpredictable. Between 1963 and 1979 there were three governments, established by three coups, whose policies were basically to spend the resources, including foreign loans, in a losing public sector. As private invest- ment receded, the public sector expanded and became the main user of growing external debt.

In the following sections, the inflow of foreign loans and their uses will be discussed and the consequences will be studied in a historical perspective. In view of political disruptions in Peru, the period under study is divided into two parts, 1963–68 and 1968–79, for the purpose of this analysis.*

THE PERIOD 1963–68

A military coup in 1962 was followed by the election of Fernando Belaunde Terry as the president of the Republic of Peru on July 28, 1963. A decree, passed by the military junta, had already established a national planning system for the economic and social development of the country. Two major organizational units, among others, were devel- oped through the decree: the National Economic and Social Development Council (CNDES) and the National Planning Institute (NPI). The CNDES, presided over by the presi- dent of Peru, became mainly responsible to formulate the government's economic and social development policies, approve the periodic plans proposed by the National Plan- ning Institute, and approve the financing alternatives of the accepted projects. The NPI, as the technical and coordinating organization of the new planning system, was basically responsible to propose and develop the planning alternatives and provide technical instructions to the re- gional planning officers throughout the country.

In July 1963, the NPI, with the cooperation of the U.S. Agency for International Development (AID), prepared a document known as the "Diagnosis," in which the economic problems of Peru and its future directions were de- scribed.[23] The "Diagnosis" was a major comprehensive

---

*Because the military coup of October 1968 was a turning point in the political and economic directions of Peru, dividing the study period at that juncture is historically justified.

economic package on which Belaunde based his initial economic policy. The main objectives of Belaunde's economic
policy were to create economic stability, strengthen the
value of the Peruvian sol, and attract foreign capital
through loans and direct investment. (The author will
discuss shortly that while the Belaunde administration was
successful in attracting foreign capital [loans], it failed to
achieve its economic goals.)

In the year Belaunde assumed office, Peru was still
suffering from uncertainty about its political direction, a
high inflation rate of about 40 to 50 percent, overcapacity
in various industries, and increasing high rates of return
on real estate speculation. Despite this gloomy picture,
investment in the private sector was still rising.[24] The
trend reversed from that in 1963 when the new government,
under the slogan "El Peru construye" (Peru builds),
launched its first huge public investment program with the
objective of building an industrial base. This was a major
turning point in the history of government policy in Peru,
the implications of which are helpful in understanding why
the Peruvian external borrowings are disassociated (or
poorly correlated) with a desired economic performance.

In an attempt to build an industrial base, Belaunde
ordered the NPI in 1963 to prepare immediately a sizable
two-year public investment program that would be financed
mainly from external sources. This public program, compatible with public opinion in the beginning of his presi-
dency, was at least politically justified. The Program of
Public Investment for Peru (1964–65) was prepared by the
NPI and approved by the CNDES in 1964. The whole
package was immediately submitted to the Inter-American
Committee of the Alliance for Progress (CIAP) in October
1964. This was the first plan that the government adopted
basically from the "Diagnosis." The reason Peru involved
international organizations in the process was to obtain
their approval of the program and to encourage private and
public lending institutions to participate in financing the
proposed projects.

Representatives from various international organizations
participated in the CIAP meeting to discuss the program.
Among the participants were representatives from the U.S.
Agency for International Development, the International
Monetary Fund, the International Bank for Reconstruction
and Development, the Pan American Sanitary Bureau
(PASB), and the Panel of Nine. The representatives
unanimously supported the plan and endorsed the recom-
mendation of the IMF, which in a concluding remark,
strongly urged the Peruvian authorities to carry on their

economic and social development plan. Meantime, the IMF made standby arrangements to ensure the stability of the external balance of Peru.[25]

After the conference the external debt inflow to Peru phenomenally increased. The data in Table 4–8 indicate that the annual disbursed debt surged to $217.5 million in 1966, compared to only $53.9 in 1963—an increase equal to the annual growth rate of disbursed debt of about 100 percent in 1963–66. Note that the share of private lenders was very sizable. In 1966, about 74 percent of the disbursed loans were financed by private lenders. This simply means that the Belaunde administration succeeded in generating confidence in its public program, even among private lenders in the international capital markets.

An important point to mention is that the exclusive user of foreign loans in 1964–68 was the public sector. Although it was stated that the "need to expand public expenditures must be met in a manner compatible with the existence of a very dynamic private sector,"[26] the private sector started to collapse, in contrast to the expansion of the public sector. The private sector, in total, not only did not use any foreign finance but transferred a surplus fund of 3.5 percent of the GDP to the public sector. In 1964–68, the public sector, with a negative savings (loss) of -.4 percent of the GDP, absorbed all the imported loans. The volume of public investments rose to 5 percent of the GDP in 1964–68, compared to 3.6 percent in the previous period. Meantime, the volume of private investments decreased to 13.2 percent of the GDP, compared to a previous level of 17.5 percent.[27]

After rising public expenditures and declining private investments, Peru ran into a debt and economic crisis that started in 1966–67. The GDP growth started to decline and the trade deficit started to rise.

With respect to the return on public investments, the public sector, with minus savings, did not contribute a single sol to the surplus in the economy. This is partly understandable because public investments were allocated mainly to the infrastructure sectors: roads, ports and airports, irrigation, housing, health, and water and energy. The share of industry was minimal. However, the Belaunde administration ignored the fact that public expenditures, which were sizably financed by the imported loans, had to be matched by a certain level of public revenue. Failure to realize this fact, coupled with the collapse of private investments in the same period, are among the reasons for the economic crisis of 1966–67, after aggressive borrowing during the Belaunde administration.

E. V. K. Fitzgerald, who was a top consultant to the NPI, critically argued that the public investment program was not an actual plan, that the "plans" were basically made up to satisfy the aid agencies.[28]   V. Roeal also believed that the basic objective of the plan was to "solicit the financial services" of the Alliance for Progress in the process of borrowing from abroad. He made a harsh criticism of the plan, that even ". . . no Minister, nor the President of the Republic, nor the Congress, base their decision on it."[29]

Parallel with rising public expenditures, the external debt outstanding for Peru was mounting, and it reached $634 million disbursed and $1 billion including undisbursed in 1967. The debt service obligations, expressed as a percentage of exports, grew from 7 percent in 1965 to 15 percent in 1968.[30]   This financial pressure was unprecedented in Peru, and it was very alarming for a borrowing LDC whose imported loans were aggressively spent mainly for social overhead. Faced with a rising external gap and a rising budget deficit, the Belaunde administration announced a 40 percent devaluation of the sol, new tariffs on imports, and a series of budget cuts and credit restrictions in 1967. In fact, this effort was made as a precondition to obtain a $43 million credit from the IMF to relieve temporarily the mounting debt pressure. The international lending institutions responded to the crisis by a sharp decline in their lending to Peru. Official loans and private loans dropped by 16 and 28 percent, respectively, in 1967 (see Table 4-8).

Meantime, the government of Peru started to negotiate with the creditors for the rescheduling of outstanding loans and debt services. However, the creditors were unwilling to reschedule the due payments until the government presented a realistic projection of its future revenues for the payment of debt services. The Central Bank of Peru developed a prospectus in which future payments would be generated out of the proceeds of the investments in copper mines in the near future.

The task of rescheduling, which preoccupied the administration throughout 1968, was neither an easy process nor a fundamental solution to the economic crisis of Peru. Various creditors were involved, and each creditor had a different view about the rescheduling. Creditors in the United States were either the U.S. government (AID and the Export-Import Bank) or the commercial banks. The U.S. government loans had such a high grant element (concession) that the rescheduling was not economically justified. The commercial banks in the United States,

TABLE 4-8. External Debt Inflow to Peru (millions of U.S. dollars)

	1963	1964	1965	1966	1967	1968	1969	1970	1971
Total Disbursements	53.9	83.4	137.8	217.5	164.1	176.4	164.6	147.8	147.6
Official loans				56.1	47.2	53.0	54.7	59.4	85.9
(Portion of total disbursements)				26%	29%	30%	33%	40%	58%
Multilateral				22.0	24.6	10.7	15.1	17.9	19.8
Bilateral				34.1	22.6	42.3	39.6	41.5	66.1
Private loans				161.4	116.9	123.4	109.9	88.4	61.7
(Portion of total disbursements)				74%	71%	70%	67%	60%	42%
Suppliers									
Financial markets									
Annual growth rates									
Official loans					-16%	12%	3%	9%	45%
Private loans					-28%	6%	-11%	-20%	-30%
Net resource transfer on account of annual debt	14.0	41.5	86.5	132.0	70.5	38.9	47.2	4.3	21.7

94

	1972	1973	1974	1975	1976	1977	1978	1979
Total Disbursements	278.8	668.1	1,083.2	1,067.6	935.9	1,286.0	841.7	1,631.7
Official loans	105.1	163.6	334.6	439.4	358.8	710.4	485.8	459.9
(Portion of total disbursements)	38%	24%	31%	41%	38%	55%	58%	28%
Multilateral	10.5	9.4	10.9	17.4	25.9	60.5	49.2	98.0
Bilateral	94.6	154.2	323.7	422.0	332.9	649.9	436.6	361.9
Private loans	173.7	504.4	748.6	628.2	577.1	575.6	355.9	1,171.8
(Portion of total disbursements)	62%	76%	69%	59%	62%	45%	42%	72%
Suppliers		104.0	124.4	165.2	134.4	129.8	181.1	143.0
Financial markets		400.4	624.2	463.0	442.7	445.8	174.8	1,028.8
Annual growth rates								
Official loans	122%	56%	105%	31%	-18%	98%	-32%	-5%
Private loans	182%	190%	48%	-16%	8%	0%	-38%	229%
Net resource transfer on account of annual debt	96.4	270.1	651.3	631.3	481.7	634.0	93.7	328.9

Source: World Bank, World Debt Tables.

95

which were the deposit holders of the Central Bank of Peru, had more at stake in the rescheduling proposal submitted by Peru. Therefore they were relatively more flexible in preventing a balance of payment crisis.

The situation was different in Europe and Japan, where the final decision had to be made jointly by government agencies and the commercial banks. Furthermore, the lenders in Europe were from different nations—Belgium, Finland, Germany, Italy, Spain, and the United Kingdom. Added to all those complexities was the Peruvian lack of experience in rescheduling foreign loans.[31]

The results of the negotiations were a debt rescheduling relief in 1968 and another debt rescheduling in 1969. As pointed out, the debt rescheduling could not be a final solution to the economic problem of Peru. Peru had to make up the debt relief within a period of only two years. For instance, Peru had to pay more than $20 million, above the original debt services, in 1970. The assumption behind the rescheduling was that Peru would be able to bear the additional pressure of the rescheduled debt services in the short run. This assumption was unrealistic, as Peru was suffering from a multifaceted crisis in which mining production, the major source of exports, was stagnant; the future of export revenues depended mainly on the fluctuation of international prices; public investments, in which all foreign loans were spent, were operating at a loss; foreign investment inflows were insufficient to meet the rising external gap; government expenditures were not politically easy to halt; and the private sector was still passive and unclear about the true attitude of the government toward private investment.

Throughout 1963–68, private investors at home and abroad followed the controversial issue of the International Petroleum Company (IPC) as a major indicator of the government's attitude toward private investment.[32] However, the position of the government toward IPC was vague until the last days before its collapse. In June 1965, the national convention of the Accion Popular party, whose original founder was Belaunde, voted to expropriate IPC. However, Belaunde neither reversed nor implemented the voted proposal. In this vague and unpredictable atmosphere, the natural response was a declining rate of private investment.

In the midst of the public investment program, which was tied to the inflow of external loans, the president of the Board of Governors of the Central Bank in Peru warned that the extension of the government credit violated the IMF's original agreement. This man, who was an outspoken critic of public expenditures, in his letter of resignation warned of the unpleasant consequences of the overspending of the loans in a losing public sector that would create further deficits.[33] This view became fact in the debt and economic crisis of 1966–68.

In October 1968, at the peak of the economic and political crisis, Belaunde was ousted from his office through a military coup led by General Velasco.

THE PERIOD 1968–79

In the early years of the Velasco government, the external borrowing of Peru declined from $176.4 million in 1968 to $147.6 million in 1971. A major portion of the new loans was used to pay the debt services of the previous loans whose payments had been rescheduled for the early years of the 1970s. Therefore the net resource transfer on account of annual borrowing declined and reached its lowest record of only $4.3 million in 1970 (see Table 4–8). Private loans had negative growth rates of -11, 120, and -30 percent in 1969, 1970, and 1971, respectively.

Explanations for the declining trend in borrowing in 1968 to 1971 are as follows: First, on taking power in October 1968, Velasco inherited an economy deflated by the impact of the devaluation of the sol, import restrictions, and some budget cuts in 1967. Such a deflationary course was further strengthened by the new government through a 10 percent surcharge on all private sector imports. More restrictions on bank credits, government consumption, and public investments were exercised until 1971. The effect was, temporarily, a positive balance of payments and a lower demand for foreign loans.

The second reason for a decline in debt inflow was that the new government, immediately one month after the takeover, expropriated the International Petroleum Corporation, without compensation, and converted it into a state oil company named Petroperu. Cerro de Pasco, the major mining company, was also expropriated and renamed Centromine. Marconona, which was a major company in ore operation, became a national company, Hierroperu. A subsidiary of ITT and a Swedish company was nationalized and became a state enterprise, Entelperu. A British railway company was nationalized and renamed Enafer. Financial institutions, including such foreign banks as Continental of Chase Manhattan, Lima of France, and Credito of Italy, were all nationalized. Grace Corporation, a major foreign company in the sugar industry, was completely taken over by the government.[34] All these expropriations led to intense disputes between the governments of the United States and European countries versus the Velasco government about compensation.

The immediate response of the financial community was a negative or at best a cautious attitude toward the new regime, which manifested itself in a decline in the external loans to Peru until 1971 (see Table 4–8). However, during this short period of declining borrowing, Peru maintained a solvent economy compared to the previous years. This temporary phenomenon is partially explained by the deflationary policy of the new government that had been in effect since the last two years of the previous regime. In the stagnant period of the external debt inflow (1967–71), the trade balance was positive, and the GDP growth, despite its fluctuation, was also positive. The positive trade balance, however, was due to the rise of international prices rather than any significant increase in the volume of exports.[35]

The favorable economic situation and the stagnant period of external borrowing were temporary and did not last beyond 1971. The savings of the state enterprises, which became the major focus of the new government policy for growth, started to decline from 1971 and reached a negative value. Meantime, private investment sharply declined and remained stagnant in the early 1970s.

In view of the deterioration of both public savings and private savings, the Peruvian economy seriously needed a new source of financing. The intensity of this financial need is reflected in the economic plan of 1970–75, through which the annual growth rates of public investment were projected at about 40 percent, mainly in industry and mineral. The achievement of such planned rates of growth, in the light of declining public and private surpluses, obviously required imported foreign currency. In the 1970–75 economic plan there was a shift in the economic policy, with emphasis of investments directed toward minerals.[36] First, one could predict from the beginning that Peru, no matter how radical it became in 1969, would finally have to take recourse in the international financial markets to finance at least part of its state projects. Second, the imported foreign loans would be spent more aggressively than before in the public sector, and the private sector would further lose its role in the economy.

Going to the international financial markets finally occurred in February 1972, when the Consultative Group of the creditors was reconvened under the direction of the International Bank for Reconstruction and Development, after being inactive for about six years, to consider the new economic package of the Velasco regime. This was the major sign that Peru needed a substantial amount of foreign currency. The results of this meeting were preliminary agreements with several countries for a credit of well over $400 million to finance state projects, including the Cerro Verde copper mine, the IPC copper refinery, and a fertilizer plant.[37] This recourse to foreign lenders is reflected in Table 4–8, which shows that annual disbursed loans started to increase again in 1972. Private loans increased by 182 and 190 percent in 1972 and 1973, respectively. In fact, the inflow of external funds to Peru did not resume until the government made some compromise and showed some flexibility in negotiations over expropriated foreign capital.

Other events also encouraged the international financial community to participate aggressively in financing the development plans of Peru after 1972. First, Peru had a plan to invest the imported loans in the exploration and extraction of oil and copper and other minerals through newly formed state enterprises. Second, the price of oil started to rise in the world market and, at the same time, the copper industry in neighboring Chile was nationalized and its future supply became uncertain. These events, coupled with a surplus of petrodollars in the market, led to the resumption of external loans, particularly of private loans, to Peru after a moratorium on borrowing.

Fitzgerald reports that during 1974–76, the value of projects listed for foreign finance exceeded $3 billion.[38] Amazon oil exploration, Cerro Verde Copper Refinery, Talara Refinery, Illo Copper Refinery, other oil operations, and a series of irrigation projects absorbed a portion of the imported loans. Also, the public sector grew substantially, reaching a spectacular 9.2 percent of the GDP during 1974–76. More than half of public investment was financed by foreign capital. In 1974, annual disbursed loans to Peru reached a record high of $1,083.2 million, out of which the share of the private lenders was about 69 percent (see Table 4–8). Private loans, from various countries, including the United States, Japan, and European countries, rose significantly to $748.6 million in 1974.

COFIDE, the state international financing intermediary in Peru, aggressively tapped all possible private and public sources in the world to finance the state projects and government expenditures. This phenomenon was not surprising in the case of the expropriation and domination of the public sector. Stated simply, the Velasco administration did not extend any assured invitation to either domestic or foreign private investors; therefore the private sector remained very passive in that period.

Consequently, in 1974, the state enterprises were less than successful and the economy in general was moving toward a new crisis, similar to that of the mid-1960s. Just as the previous administration had begun successfully and then ran into a serious problem, so did the Velasco government. After a short period during which the country enjoyed a rising GDP and an improving external gap in the early 1970s, the GDP started to decline. During this time, Peru experienced also a widening trade deficit and deteriorating savings.

There are at least two interrelated explanations for this unfavorable outcome. First, the public enterprises in which the foreign loans were spent yielded either negative savings or a very low surplus after 1973. Second, the investments in the oil and copper industries were estimated too optimistically. Simply stated, the public sector, on which the borrowing policy was based, did not perform well, as its returns did not compensate the cost of borrowing in the mid-1970s. Petroperu, the major state oil company, absorbed part of the external loans for its investments. However, Petroperu operated at a loss, at least until 1978, because the revenue of the products sold on the domestic market did not cover the production costs.[39] The government had a social policy to subsidize oil prices. The irony was that the government could never afford to pay the cost of the subsidies to Petroperu. The result was that about 8.3 billion soles of the uncollected subsidies was still on the balance sheet of the company until 1978.[40] This, in fact, means that the government borrowed from abroad to finance part of its social program.

Mineroperu, Centromine, and Hierroperu are the three major enterprises that constitute the mining industry. Their exports accounted for more than 60 percent of the export revenue. They were also among the recipients of external loans. With respect to their performance, these companies were operating excessively below their potential capacity at least until 1977. The reason is multifaceted, including the world recession, poor state planning, overly optimistic projections, underestimation of costs, and frequent labor strikes in the mid-1970s.

The government expected the Cerro Verde mines to be in operation in 1975. However, the project did not start to produce until 1977–78. And the other major project, the Canjone mines, did not start to produce until late 1976. The Amazon oil fields were much less successful than anticipated. In 1974, it was discovered that the oil reserves had been significantly overestimated. The revenues from the oil reserves had been projected to enable the government to pay the rising debt services as the oil prices were rising. This did not come true, as the oil extracted barely exceeded domestic consumption in the mid-1970s.

Failure of public planning and public investments in petroleum and copper is well illustrated (see Table 4–9). The figures in the table indicate that the export of copper and petroleum was almost stagnant until 1977. The state copper and petroleum industries, the two major potential sources to pay the debt services and improve the trade deficit, did not generate enough export revenues as it was ambitiously projected in the early 1970s. In fact, any minimal increases in the export revenues from petroleum and copper were realized because of rising prices rather than increasing outputs. This is reflected in a declining index for the volume of exports and an increasing index for the unit price of exports (see *International Financial Statistics*).

Faced with the reality that the government projects were too optimistic, Peru had no alternative but to scrap a lot of the projects in the mid-1970s. A costly state project, which had been planned to extend a trans-Andean pipeline, was stopped when it was discovered that the Amazon oil fields did not have sufficient oil reserves. Further exploration for oil reserves needed more financing beyond an already huge sunk cost. The facts that the major projects did not pay off as planned, and government expenditures grew phenomenally, brought on the economic crisis. The government, which was dominating the economy, made a tenfold budget deficit from 3.2 billion soles in 1970 to 30.5 billion soles in 1975.[41]

Peru ran into a huge trade deficit of 8.2 percent of the GDP in 1975. Thus the basic purpose of its external borrowing became to offset the deficit in the balance of payments. In 1975, Peru had to borrow more than $1 billion to maintain the balance of payments and keep the economy running. In the same year, outstanding debt reached more than $3 billion, with more than $500 million worth of servicing. In the light of a stagnant volume of exports, a rising trade deficit, a rising government deficit, a stagnant private sector, deteriorating savings of the public enterprises, and a declining GDP, the case of Peru became very alarming in the financial community in 1975. It became obvious that the public programs, to which most of the available resources, including foreign loans, had been rechanneled, were a failure.

A cut in the export production created rising unemployment, labor strikes, and political uncertainty. The situation became more tense when the government started to

TABLE 4-9. Export Performance of Copper and Petroleum

	Export Revenue from Copper (billions of Soles)	Export Revenue from Petroleum (millions of U.S. dollars)
1969	9.05	6
1970	10.04	8
1971	10.42	6
1972	6.58	8
1973	7.30	4
1974	11.10	3
1975	13.46	21
1976	6.16	29
1977	13.03	39
1978	30.45	180
1979	65.49	477

Source: International Financial Statistics Yearbook (Washington, D.C.: International Monetary Fund 1981); Latin American Economic Report, July 13, 1979, 214.

retreat gradually from its social programs and raise food and oil prices, which had been heavily subsidized since 1969. Taxes were also raised to help offset the government deficits. The result was further strikes and riots, which finally brought the Velasco regime to a collapse. In August 1975, Velasco was removed from office and Morales Bermudez became the new president.

The basic philosophy of the Bermudez government was that the exclusive allocation of the resources to the public sector would not bring the desired economic growth. His program included a series of reforms, beginning with tax increases, further elimination of the subsidies, stricter control on imports, curtailment of wage increases, and encouragement of the small and medium-sized private enterprises to resume investments. Yet the private sector wanted further concessions to participate in the domestic capital formation. The middle-ground position of Bermudez toward the private sector did not satisfy either the business group or organized labor and the radical elements. His policies were negated by the passiveness of the private sector on the one hand and frequent strikes by labor on the other.

Peru was at the peak of its political and economic uncertainty in 1975–76. Suffering from a chronic shortage of foreign exchange reserves and a deteriorating balance of payments, Peru took recourse in the IMF, in the early part of 1976, for a credit support. At this juncture, the IMF was in a position to impose policy conditions on Peru before extending its own resources and/or assuring the international community of the future solvency of that country. It was, in fact, because of the IMF conditions that Peru devaluated the sol by 44 percent, further cut public expenditures, lifted its subsidy program for petroleum and foodstuffs, and curtailed wage increases in and after 1976. The IMF, in exchange, supported Peru in obtaining some loans from private lenders in the United States and Europe, including a credit for $240 million from a group led by Wells Fargo and another $100 million from a European consortium, at market rates, during the peak of the crisis. These credits were to be renewed if the economic performance of Peru became normal.[42]

However, the balance of payments did not improve after the IMF intervention, and the growth rates of the GDP reached their lowest levels of 1.2 percent in 1977 and -3 percent in 1978. The annual debt services rose to $651 million in 1977 and $748 million in 1978, bringing the debt service ratios to the alarming levels of 30.5 percent and 31.3 percent in those two years, respectively.[43]

The international financial community was discouraged by the Peruvian economic performance. Meantime, Peru was at the mercy of the IMF, either to accept the stabilization program in its full implementation or to face the risk and consequences of a default. Yet Peru was still resisting a full capitulation to the IMF.

In November 1977, the IMF and Peru finally signed a standby agreement for $100 million for a period of two years through which Peru became obliged to follow the policy direction of the IMF. Even with the IMF credit, Peru realized that it still had a major gap between its available credits and the government expenditures and imports. In February 1978 a group of Peruvian representatives went to New York, Paris, Frankfurt, San Francisco, and Tokyo to discuss a new loan package. The Peruvian group was able to secure promises from the banks, although reluctantly, to put up $260 million, tied to the IMF "austerity agreement" of November 1977. All these credits were contingent upon the periodic auditing of the Peruvian accounts by the IMF authorities.

A month after obtaining the reluctant promises from the private banks, Peru was confronted with a fraud. Inspectors from the IMF came to Lima to make certain that the obtained credits were spent according to the provisions of the austerity program. Unexpectedly, they found that the central bank has been "cooking" most of the figures. International reserves were maintained over the new year by a $40 million four-day loan from a Dresdner Bank subsidiary. The budget deficit, planned at $125 million, had been overspent in the first two months of the year.[44]

Thus the stability program of Peru turned out to be a scandal. In March 1978 the IMF closed its standby agreement with Peru and deprived it of drawing IMF funds. The commercial banks, with a sizable debt services due, were faced with a dilemma—whether to offer the previously promised credits to Peru or to force Peru to capitulate completely to the IMF in further negotiations. The steering committee of the bankers, including Manufacturers Hanover (chair), Citibank, Wells Fargo, Dresdner Bank of Europe (representing Europeans), the Bank of Tokyo, and the Bank of Nova Scotia, gathered to discuss Peru.[45] The result was not to extend the loans, going along with the IMF's refusal.

Consequently, the annual debt disbursed to Peru significantly declined by 32 percent in official loans and 38 percent in private loans. Also, in 1977–78, private capital had a substantial outflow due to the economic and political uncertainty that was dominating the country during the crisis. Private investment, due to uncertainty, and public investment, due to lack of finance and some deflationary policies, substantially decreased. In fact, the economy was at a complete recess, with huge external debt services due to both private and public lenders. The public investments in operation were still losing in 1977–78.

Consistent with the above analysis is the description of the economy of Peru in 1978 by Javier Silva Ruete, minister of economy and finance, that the balance of trade was negative, national income was 40 percent below the level of 1975, reserves had a deficit of $1.25 billion, and the rate of inflation was close to 100 percent.[46]

CONCLUSION

The main conclusion from the case studies of Korea and Peru is that the basic purpose of external borrowing for Korea was to build an industrial base in general and strengthen the export sector in particular. Spending external loans in infrastructure and industrial sectors on the one hand and implementing various industrial policies on the other tend to explain, among other things, the unique association of the Korean debt with the values of its economic performance. The unfavorable economic performance of Peru, in the aftermath of aggressive borrowing can be attributed to the spending of most resources, including foreign loans, in a losing public sector. Therefore the purpose and uses of borrowing in Peru, unlike in the case of Korea, have been to finance a losing public sector and consequently to finance a deteriorating balance of payments.[47] In other words, the motivation of borrowing in Peru, unlike Korea, was to finance a nonproductive sector and maintain balance of payments. This motivation, among other things, tends to explain the unfavorable correlation between Peruvian borrowing and the values of its economic performance.

NOTES

1. For an interesting presentation of the historical events, see L. L. Wade and B. S. Kim, *Economic Development of South Korea: The Political Economy of Success* (New York: Praeger, 1978).

2. United Nations, *Summaries of the Industrial Development Plans of Thirty Countries* 1 (Vienna: UNIDO, 1975).

3. Wade and Kim, *Economic Development of South Korea,* p. 205.

4. Larry E. Westphal, "Korean Development: More to It Than Meets the Eye," unpublished paper, p. 1.

5. Leroy P. Jones and Il Sakong, *Government, Business and Entrepreneurship in Economic Development: The Case of Korea* (Cambridge, Mass.: Harvard University Press, 1980), p. 3.

6. Wade and Kim interestingly comment that "an explanation of Korean development will require the collaborative effort . . . of sociologists, anthropologists, psychologists, political scientists, economists and historians, and it is even then likely that no explanation will be forthcoming in which all contributing factors are precisely weighted and integrated into an arguable theoretical statement" (Wade and Kim, *Economic Development of South Korea,* p. 205).

7. Anne O. Krueger, *The Developmental Role of the Foreign Sector and Aid* (Cambridge, Mass.: Harvard University Press, 1979), Tables 30, 31, pp. 109, 113.

8. Charles R. Frank et al., *Foreign Trade Regimes and Economic Development: South Korea* (New York: Columbia University Press, 1975), p. 104.

9. Krueger, *The Developmental Role of the Foreign Sector and Aid,* p. 144.

10. For comparative rates on domestic and foreign loans, see Wontack Hong, "Trade, Distortions and Employment

Growth in Korea," mimeograph (Seoul: Korean Development Institute, 1977), statistical appendix, Table 4.8; and Frank et al., *Foreign Trade Regimes,* p. 116. A summary of both is presented in Krueger, *The Developmental Role of the Foreign Sector and Aid,* p. 175.

11. Frank et al., *Foreign Trade Regimes,* p. 117.

12. *International Financial Statistics* (Washington, D.C.: International Monetary Funds, 1982).

13. Wade and Kim, *Economic Development of South Korea,* pp. 228–29.

14. Republic of Korea, *Summary of the First Five-Year Economic Plan (1962–1966)* (Seoul, 1962), pp. 24–25, Table 4.

15. Ibid., p. 29.

16. Republic of Korea, *Summary of the Second Five-Year Economic Plan (1967–1971)* (Seoul, 1967), appendix table 22, p. 16.

17. Irma Adelman, *Practical Approaches to Development Planning: Korea's Second Five-Year Plan* (Baltimore: Johns Hopkins University Press, 1969), p. 5.

18. Frank et al., *Foreign Trade Regimes,* pp. 52–53, Table 4.2.

19. Kwang Suk Kim, "Outward-Looking Industrialization: The Case of Korea," in Wontack Hong and Anne O. Krueger, *Trade and Development in Korea* (Seoul: Korean Development Institute, 1975), pp. 25–26.

20. An Export Day was also established on November 30, 1964, when Korea celebrated the first $100 million export market in its history. On November 30 of every year exporters with the best performance receive "industrial merit-medals" of gold, silver, and bronze directly from the president. See Jones and Sakong, *Government, Business and Entrepreneurship,* pp. 98, 403.

21. Republic of Korea, *Summary of the Third Five-Year Economic Development Plan (1972–1976)* (Seoul, 1971), pp. 6–7.

22. Republic of Korea, *Summary of the Fourth Five-Year Economic Development Plan (1977–1981)* (Seoul, 1976), pp. 7–8.

23. The joint study consisted of six volumes of more than 1,500 pages. Each volume was allocated for a specific economic or social issue. See Daniel R. Kitty, *Planning for Development in Peru* (New York: Praeger, 1967), pp. 71–79.

24. Private fixed investments, as a percentage of the GDP, were 16.0, 17.8, and 19.0 in 1960, 1961, and 1962, respectively. See Pedro-Pablo Kuczynski, *Peruvian Democracy Under Economic Stress* (Princeton, N.J.: Princeton

University Press, 1977), p. 59, Table 10.

25. Organization of American States, Inter-American Economic and Social Council, *Final Act of the CIAP Subcommittee on Peru* (Washington, D.C., 1964), p. 6.

26. Ibid., p. 12.

27. E. V. K. Fitzgerald, *The Political Economy of Peru 1956–1978* (Cambridge: Cambridge University Press, 1979), p. 162, Table 6.4.

28. E. V. K. Fitzgerald, *The State and Economic Development: Peru Since 1968* (Cambridge: Cambridge University Press, 1976), p. 79.

29. Ibid., pp. 78–79. The original document is V. Roeal, *La Planification Economica en el Peru* (Lima, 1968).

30. International Bank for Reconstruction and Development, *The Current Economic Position and Prospects of Peru* (Washington, D.C., 1973), p. 42.

31. See Kuczynski, *Peruvian Democracy,* pp. 252–53.

32. IPC, which operated in several Latin American countries, was a completely owned subsidiary of Standard Oil of New Jersey. It produced more than 50 percent of the total oil output of Peru in the 1960s. The dispute between the government and IPC had both economic and political implications. Some suggest that the removal of Belaunde from office was the immediate reaction of the nationalist militarists to Belaunde's agreement with IPC on August 12, 1968. For details of the case, see A. J. Pinelo, *The Multinational Corporation as a Force in Latin American Politics: A Case Study of the IPC* (New York: Praeger, 1973).

33. Kitty, *Planning for Development in Peru,* p. 110.

34. Fitzgerald, *The State and Economic Development,* p. 29.

35. The point can be verified through the price index and the volume index of exports in Peru in *International Financial Statistics* (Washington, D.C., International Monetary Fund, 1972).

36. Institute for National Planning, *Plan del Peru 1971–1975* (Lima, 1971).

37. International Bank for Reconstruction and Development, *Current Economic Position,* p. 43.

38. Fitzgerald, *The State and Economic Development,* p. 89.

39. The cost of petroleum was 120 soles, and it was being sold at 80 soles, which meant a 40-sol subsidy. See the interview with Alvaro Meneses, president of Banco de la Nacion of Peru, in *Euromoney,* June 1980, p. 32.

40. "Wealth Flows Over the Andeas," in "Peru—A Survey," *Euromoney* June 1980, p. 22.

41. International Monetary Fund, *International Financial Statistics Yearbook* (Washington, D.C., 1981).

42. The process of negotiations and the IMF conditions for a stability program are presented in Rosemary Thorp and Lawrence Whitehead, *Inflation and Stabilization in Latin America* (New York: Holmes and Meier, 1979).

43. World Bank, *World Debt Tables* (EC-167/80) (Washington, D.C., 1980).

44. "Peru: Back to Crisis," *The Economist* 266 (March 1978): 77–78.

45. Ibid.

46. Javier Silva Ruete, "Something Had to Be Done to Rescue the Country," in "Peru—A Survey," *Euromoney,* June 1980, p. 4. The economy could operate in 1978, mainly through the selling of some gold, $25 million loan from Venezuela, $15 million loan from each of Spain, Brazil, and Mexico; and $1 million from even the "tiny" Dominican Republic! See "Manual Moroyra, the Tough Negotiator," in "Peru—A Survey," *Euromoney,* June 1980, p. 28.

47. It was known in 1977 that part of the purpose of external borrowing in recent years had been to purchase substantial arms from the USSR! See "From Down to Lower," *Euromoney,* May 1978, p. 62.

5
Summary
and Conclusions

This study is part of the empirical literature on external finance and development. Its purpose was basically to determine If a higher level of external borrowing is associated with more favorable values of economic growth for borrowing LDCs. The inflow of external debt has not been of the same magnitude for all borrowing LDCs. Some LDCs, relative to the size of their economies, borrowed from abroad more than others. In the light of this fact, the following hypothesis, formulated in a comparative context, was offered: A higher level of external debt capital inflow is associated with relatively more favorable values for economic growth indicators of a developing country over the long run, that is, a borrowing LDC with a higher level of external debt inflow, compared to an LDC with a lower level of debt inflow, maintains more favorable economic growth indicators in the same period of external borrowing.

A relationship between the inflow of external capital and the values of economic growth, as embodied in the hypothesis, is justified by the normative theories of external finance. The Alter aid-requirement model, the two-gap theory, and the debt cycle theory—all consistently suggest that external capital, in the form of either loans or equity, will supplement domestic resources in the process of economic development. Thus the interaction between external finance and development is conceptually meaningful.

Although a few studies raised this inquiry for individual countries, there was no study for a group of LDCs in a comparative context. Therefore 20 borrowing LDCs were selected for study. Members of OPEC, centrally planned economies, higher income group countries and lower income group countries were excluded. The time period under study was 1963 to 1979. Nine economic indicators were used as indices of economic growth: incremental capital output ratio (ICOR), the marginal savings ratio, the average savings ratio, the growth rate of export, the growth rate of GDP, the ratio of export to GDP, the external gap (exports–imports), the internal gap (savings–investment), and the net resource transfer on account of debt capital. The theoretical/conceptual validity of these indices was supported (see appendix).

To investigate the validity of the hypothesis, a research question was raised: Between two countries with similar equity capital inflow, but different levels of external borrowing, did the country with a higher level of external borrowing maintain more favorable growth indicators during a specified period of borrowing? In the process of pairing a high-borrowing country with a low-borrowing country, the countries in the sample were ranked according to their average annual monetary values of direct investment and average annual monetary values of external borrowing, adjusted for size of their economies. Using bivariate analysis (paired t-test), seven pairs of borrowing LDCs were selected after a series of trial and error. As a result, the countries in each pair had significantly different levels of external borrowing and similar (insignificantly different) levels of direct investment on the average annual basis.

The values of economic growth indicators were computed for the countries in each pair for 1965 to 1979. With respect to individual economic indicators, paired t-tests were run to determine if the average annual values were significantly different between a high-borrowing country versus a low-borrowing country in each pair. The results of these tests were summarized and presented in Tables 3–4, 3–5, and 3–6. Of 56 tests, only 16 showed that the differences in the values of economic indicators were in favor of the high-borrowing countries. There was no pattern for even a specific indicator to be consistently in favor of the high-borrowing countries (see Table 3–5). Except for Korea, whose results were exceptional, only 9 tests out of a total of 46 showed that the values of economic indicators were in favor of the high-borrowing LDCs. More strikingly, 11 tests tended to suggest that the values of the indicators were even significantly less favorable on the part of high-borrowing countries (see Table 3–6).

In view of these results, the analysis concluded that the research hypothesis could not be confirmed. Although the obvious patterns in Tables 3–5, 3–6, and 3–7 suggested that the number of tests in support of the hypothesis was very low (9 out of 46), a dichotomous test was also made (see Table 3–8). The result was that the number of tests in support of the hypothesis was not sufficient to give a positive answer to the research question.

To verify further this conclusion, multiple regressions, both regular and logarithmic, were run for individual high-borrowing countries in the sample. The purpose of these regressions was to identify any existing relationship between the values of external borrowing (deflated dollars) and the values of four selected economic indicators—the incremental capital output ratio, the marginal savings ratio, the growth rate of exports, and the growth rate of GDP. These variables were chosen on the ground that each reflects a separate concept and varies relatively independent of the others. The results of the regressions were summarized and presented in Tables 3–9 and 3–10.

Consistent with the previous tests, the case of Korea was again exceptional. There were strong linear and logarithmic relationships between the level of the external borrowing of Korea and the values of its selected economic indicators. The coefficients of determination were .95 and .81 in linear and logarithmic functions, respectively. The F-ratios of both regressions for the case of Korea were significant at a confidence level of more than 99 percent. A surprising result was a negative sign for the variable of growth of export of Korea in the regression. The reason was a multicollinearity between the growth rate of export and the growth rate of the GDP. Once the latter variable was excluded from the regression, the sign of the growth rate in export became positive, and other statistics remained significant as before. Most of the correlation between Korean borrowing and Korean economic indicators was attributed to the growth rate of export and the growth rate of the GDP in regression analysis.

The results were different for other borrowing LDCs. The coefficient of determination ranged for .03 percent for Chile to 63 percent for Peru. Taking a 95 percent level of confidence, the F-ratio of the regression was significant only for Costa Rica. Yet the F-ratios for the coefficients of the ICOR, the growth rate of exports, and the growth rate of the GDP of Costa Rica were all insignificant at the same level of confidence. With respect to the results of logarithmic regressions, the case of Korea remained exceptional as before. The poor correlation was still true for Tunisia, Panama, and Chile. Peru and Costa Rica slightly improved with coefficients of determination of .64 and .67, respectively. The corresponding F-ratios were significant at a confidence level of more than 95 percent. Yet Peru held negative coefficients for marginal savings ratio, growth rate of the GDP, and growth rate of exports, whose values were significant for the latter variables. The case of Costa Rica could not be strongly supported because the value of R^2 was not very high (.67), the Durbin-Watson was low, and the coefficients for the growth rates of export and the GDP were insignificant.

In light of the results from the paired t-tests and regression analysis, the author could not give a positive answer to the main research question; therefore the hypothesis was not confirmed. Having determined that the level of external borrowing per se did not have a strong association with the values of economic indicators, a supplementary question was raised: What has been the motivation (purpose and uses) of the external borrowing? Did the motivation of borrowing influence the values of growth indicators? A case study approach. To carry out this supplementary inquiry, it was assumed that the government policies for borrowing and the pattern of spending of foreign loans would reflect the motivation of the borrowers. The study was done for the cases of Korea and Peru, both of which were the major borrowing LDCs in the period under study. Korea was selected because it maintained a unique association between borrowing and the values of economic performance. The selection of Peru was justified mainly because its economic performance was disassociated with its huge volumes of debt, and the size of the economy of Peru, compared to other high-borrowing LDCs, was closest to that of Korea.

The study showed that the government of Korea adopted a series of policies to encourage foreign borrowing in the mid-1960s. The loan guarantee plans, the control of interest rates, and the foreign exchange reforms served as incentives for borrowing from abroad. In fact, foreign loans, compared to domestic loans, became very economical and, in some cases, a source of economic gain. As a result, the inflow of foreign debt started to grow phenomenally from the mid-1960s. Private loans rose from $110.3 million in 1966 to $507.9 million in 1968, equal to an annual rate of increase of 90 percent. Official loans, mainly in the form of bilateral loans, also rose throughout 1966–70.

Simultaneously, the government started to offer generous incentives for the expansion of exports. Thus the policies to stimulate foreign borrowing on the one hand and the policies to promote exports on the other were tied together. The number and variety of policy reforms, which were directed toward the expansion of exports, reflected the unequivocal commitment of the Korean government for an export-led growth.

The data showed that in 1967–75 more than 60 percent of the total commercial loans were used in the manufacturing sector. Within the manufacturing sector, the shares of textiles, chemicals, petroleum, metals, nonmetals, and transportation were significant. The data published by the Economic Planning Board of Korea also indicated that the ratio of capital goods and raw materials imported for export production continuously rose from 20.6 percent in 1963 to 58.2 percent in 1977. This simply means that for every $100 foreign exchange available in 1977, about $58.2 was used for the export sector. Thus external borrowing, as a major source of foreign exchange, became a service function for the export industries. This strong motivation for export was also reflected in the objectives of the periodic five-year plans of Korea.

Important is that the motivation (borrowing for the purpose of export expansion) remained steady. In short periods of crisis the government readily reacted by special emergency decrees to alleviate problems. As example is the Emergency Presidential Decree for Economic Stabilization and Growth in 1972, which turned around a temporary decline in export production by implementing a series of corrective and incentive measures. Also, most of the export incentives established in the 1960s remained intact or were expanded throughout the 1970s.

The motivation of external borrowing was different in the case of Peru. In 1963, a two-year public program was prepared by the Belaunde administration. The public program was financed mainly by external loans. The annual disbursed debt rose to $217.5 million in 1966, compared to $53.9 million in 1963, equal to an annual rate of increase of 100 percent. In parallel with growing public programs, the volume of private investment started to decline, In 1964–68, public investments, which absorbed the major portion of foreign loans, yielded negative savings (loss). In the aftermath of rising public expenditures and declining private investment, Peru was faced with an unprecedented economic crisis in 1967–68. The GDP started to decline sharply. The trade balance, except in 1964, was negative throughout 1963–68. Meanwhile, foreign debt and its services were accumulating, and the expenditures of the public sector were rising.

In fact, the Belaunde administration failed to consider that the increasing public expenditures, mainly financed by external loans, needed a counterbalance, that is, a certain level of revenue. The result was an economic and debt crisis followed by a series of negotiations for debt rescheduling in 1968.

The situation did not improve, except temporarily, under the Velasco regime after 1968. In the early years of the Velasco regime, the external inflow of debt to Peru subsided mainly because of the expropriation of major foreign corporations. Meanwhile, the values of economic indicators were temporarily favorable, relative to the previous periods. However, the savings of the state enterprises started to decline in 1971. Having had an economic plan projecting for an annual growth rate of 38.7 percent in public investment, Peru started to borrow aggressively from private and official lenders again in 1972. In 1974, the annual disbursed loans to Peru reached a spectacular $1,083.2 million, out of which the share of private lenders was 69 percent (see Table 4-8). The main user of the imported loans was the public sector, as the private sector became more and more passive after the revolution (or coup) of 1968. The public investment expenditure grew substantially and reached an unprecedented size of 9.2 percent of the GDP in 1974-76, compared to a corresponding ratio of 4 percent in 1964-68. More than half of those public expenditures were financed by imported foreign funds.

In view of stagnant private investment and declining private savings, coupled with an outflow of private capital, the government had to accelerate further its external borrowing in order to finance rising public expenditures. The major state enterprises were either losing or yielding a very low return. Meanwhile, the government had to carry on its social programs, including subsidies for oil and food.

With a huge trade deficit, Peru had to take recourse in the IMF for credit support in 1976 and 1977. Following the conditions of the IMF, Peru devalued the sol, cut some public expenditures, and cancelled some of the program subsidies. In exchange, the IMF supported Peru to obtain a series of credit from private lenders. Despite these efforts, private investors were still hesitant to increase their investments. The imported funds were used mainly to pay the debt services and serve the needs of the public sector. In the process of auditing the "austerity program" of Peru, IMF inspectors discovered in February 1978 that Peru not only had violated the IMF conditions but had also manipulated the national accounting data by overstating foreign reserves and understating public expenditures. In 1978, the Peruvian economy was at the peak of recession with a negative trade deficit, a zero holdings of foreign currencies, and a still stagnant rate of private investment.

Based on the case studies of Korea and Peru, the author developed a corollary. Namely, the motivations (purpose and uses) of external borrowing in the cases of Korea and Peru were different. More specifically, the motivation of Korean borrowing was to support a successful export industry, whereas the motivation of Peruvian borrowing was to finance a losing public sector. Thus the different correlations/associations between debt and economic performance in the cases of Korea and Peru could be attributed to their different patterns of spending.

As a major contribution, this study has empirically revealed that capital in the form of external loans has not played its expected role as the "engine of growth" in the case of borrowing LDCs in the period of 1963 to 1979. As reported before, private and official loans were increasingly being injected into the economies of borrowing LDCs in the period under study. For instance, the ratio of annual debt (disbursed) to the GDP held an impressive range of 4 to 7 percent in the cases of Panama, Peru, Costa Rica, and Chile. Yet, strikingly, this research shows that such increasing values of debt (capital) have not been associated with favorable economic performance. If the supremacy of capital, as embodied in the literature of finance and development, were valid, the above results would be at least partially different.

True, some scholars have been suspicious of the overemphasis on capital as the condition of growth. However, this suspicion has never been promoted beyond a hypothesis. It is in fact through this empirical work that a theory has been developed. The essence of this theory is that the linkage between the level of external loans (capital) and the values of economic growth is *not* a guaranteed one in the case of borrowing LDCs.

Important is the fact that although this theory could be viewed as an intellectual challenge to the literature, this study does not reject the potential benefit of external loans to borrowing countries. The true implication of this study is that the policymakers in borrowing LDCs should carefully measure the potential benefit of an external loan package vis-à-vis its cost. The measurement of the net benefit of an external loan is possible by using a model of cost-benefit analysis to determine if the associated cost of borrowing will justify the contribution of borrowing to the economy. Conventional techniques in capital budgeting, such as the net present value and the internal rate of return, with any necessary modification, could be applied at the macro- and/or microlevel(s) to determine of the imported loans are economically justified. Despite the complexity of estimating the future income of certain projects and finding a proper discount rate, the task is still practical.

Another related implication of this study is that the spending pattern of loans, rather than the volume of loans, is the major factor in the process of development. It is not very difficult to visualize that return on a modest volume of debt capital used in a productive function will exceed return on a sizable volume of debt spent for unproductive or "prestige projects." Stated concisely, it is return on a unit of imported capital, rather than the quantity of cap- ital, that is the critical factor. The actual return on a unit of capital, in general, is a function of management of economy. Therefore, in the absence of an effective system to scrutinize, select, control, and evaluate the projects or areas in which imported capital is spent, any expected benefit from imported capital such as private and official debt is less than guaranteed.

Appendix: Justification of the Selected Variables

THE ALTER AID-REQUIREMENT MODEL

The seminal model of Gerald Alter is based on the assumption that the ultimate objective of economic development is to achieve a certain growth rate in per capita income in a period of time.[1] This target growth requires a certain amount of investment expenditures. Because the required rate of investment is higher than the rate of savings in the early stage of development, the target growth depends mainly on the extent to which a country can attract foreign capital. The amount of foreign capital should be equal to the difference between the amount of expenditure requirements and available domestic savings. Through the process of development, new investments lead to a higher national income (GNP or GDP) and subsequently to a higher rate of savings. As the rate of savings becomes equal to the rate of domestic investment, the country imports only a limited foreign capital to offset only the interest expenses of the outstanding loans. In the final stage of development, the rate of savings will reach a sufficient level to cover both the domestic investment expenditures and the debt services.

According to this analysis, the process of development depends mainly on the ability of the economy to boost the rate of savings. If the economy cannot generate sufficient savings while importing foreign capital, the target growth cannot be achieved and the economy has to depend on the inflow of further external capital. This dependency continues as long as the rate of savings does not meet the rate of investment.

In view of the above argument, the marginal savings ratio, the average savings ratio, and the GDP growth have been included in the list of economic growth indicators for the purpose of this study.

THE TWO-GAP THEORY

In the mid-1960s, Chenery and Strout,[2] after revising their previous articles about external foreign capital and economic development, offered a theoretical framework through which the foreign capital requirement and its contribution to the development process could be analyzed. Because the major capital inflow to LDCs in the postwar years was in the form of aid from developed countries, the focus of the theory was on foreign aid to LDCs. However, the two-gap theory is still a strong model, used to investigate empirically the relationship between foreign capital and growth of LDCs.

Foreign capital, according to the two-gap theory, has a dual effect on economic growth of a capital-importing country. First, it creates additional resources over the total domestic consumption. The additional resources are channeled to capital formation for production of further goods and services. Second, foreign capital improves the ability of LDCs to finance further imports of goods and services that are required for development. These goods and services can neither be produced nor substituted locally. Because LDCs are constrained by the shortage of domestic savings to finance all investment expenditures (internal gap), and because of the shortage of foreign capital to pay the import bills (external gap), foreign capital is the only source that can be used to fill these two binding gaps, Chenery and Strout argue. In the presence of these unfilled gaps, there is no guarantee that the target growth will be achieved. Therefore the GDP growth is constrained, in practice, by the inflow of foreign capital required to fill the larger of the two gaps.[3]

In a macroeconomic framework, the total expenditures (public and private) in a open economy can be simply formulated as follows:

GDP = Consumption + Investment + (Exports - Imports)   (1)

Alternatively, the total investment can be broken down into

$$GDP = Consumption + Savings \qquad (2)$$

Therefore investment and savings can be derived from Equations (1) and (2), respectively, as follows:

$$Investment = GDP - Consumption - (Exports - Imports) \quad (3)$$

$$Savings = GDP - Consumption \qquad (4)$$

In order to determine the two gaps, Equation (4) is subtracted from Equation (3) to obtain

$$Investment - Savings = Imports - Exports \qquad (5)$$

The left side of the equation is the amount of the internal gap and the right side is the amount of the external gap, which are theoretically equal.

For a better visualization of the effect of the foreign capital, in the process of filling the two gaps, on the growth of GDP, see Figure A–1. In phase 1, where there is no inflow of foreign capital, domestic savings remains equal to domestic investment. Domestic investment is thus restrained by a fixed savings ratio at a level of GDP_1. In phase 2, foreign capital, with a value equal to imports minus exports, enters the economy and raises the level of investment from Q_1 to Q_2. Assuming a constant capital output ratio in the model, the GDP moves to a higher position at GDP_2 as a result of new foreign capital and more domestic investment. In this phase, domestic investment is financed both indigenously (by domestic savings) and exogenously (by the excess of imports over exports finances through foreign capital).

Chenery and Eckstein argue that the internal gap is more binding than the external gap in the beginning of development process.[4] This is because the marginal propensity to save is so low in the early stage that it creates an internal gap that is more serious than the external gap. A better explanation for this inequality might be the fact that the predictions for these two gaps are determined by separate "behavioral" equations. In any case, the amount

Figure A–1.   Foreign Capital, Savings, Investment, and GDP

Phase 1:   No foreign capital

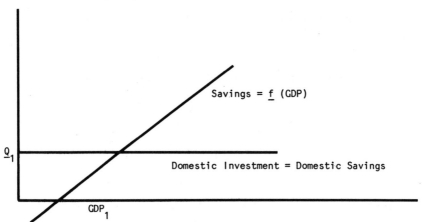

Phase 2:   Two gaps with foreign capital

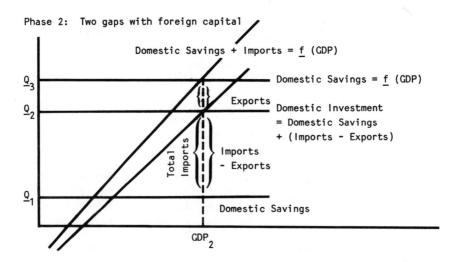

of foreign capital needed to achieve the target growth should be equal to the larger of either internal or external gap. (In the next section there is a discussion of how the values of these gaps will tend to narrow down as a result and in the process of importing foreign capital.)

Therefore both the internal gap and the external gap have been selected as proxies of economic growth in this study.

THE GROWTH-CUM-DEBT MODEL (DEBT CYCLE)

D. Avramovic, in a theoretical framework similar to that of Alter's model, suggests that "the behavior of gross capital inflow varies in different stages of what may be called the debt cycle,"[5] and the debt cycle is directly influenced by the process of importing foreign capital formation. In the first stage, when domestic resources are inadequate to finance investment expenditures, the less developed country has to borrow not only to finance the internal gap but also to repay the debt services, including interest and amortization charges. The country goes rapidly and compoundly into leverage as it has to pay back the service of the previous and new loans in order to maintain solvency for further inflows of debt in the future.

Debt inflow will assist the development in the second stage as the domestic savings ratio rises and the domestic savings supplement external capital inflow to bridge the internal gap required for the target growth. Capital formation requires the country to effect a gradual increase in its rate of savings. Because savings in the second stage are not sufficient to meet all debt services, debt would still continue to be accumulated, but at a slower pace than in the first stage. In other words, the incremental savings may cover all or part of the debt services, but the total domestic savings will still be below the total investment required for the development process. The external indebtedness rises at a diminishing rate in the latter part of the second stage so that the apogee of the curve for the debt cycle will emerge at the very end of this stage.[6] Borrowing becomes subordinate to domestic savings in bridging the investment-savings gap.

Finally, the developing borrowing country enters the third stage of the cycle when domestic savings are large enough to pay back the scheduled debt services and domestic investment expenditures. As domestic savings exceed the sum of the debt services and investment expenditures, the external borrowing progressively diminishes and "the law of compound interest now works in reverse,"[7] leading the country to a state of capital sufficiency. The country completes its debt cycle in the latter part of the third stage when it is finally in a state of self-sustained growth.

This illustration of debt cycle is merely a simplified and abstract version of a self-sustained growth process through external borrowing. In reality, many factors may lengthen the first cycle and delay the second cycle for a very long time. For instance, some countries may prefer not to pay back their debts completely even though they might have excess surplus to do so. In some cases, the capital-importing country becomes so attractive for investment that the flow of capital in the form of debt or direct investment from abroad doesn't stop. The country goes through such an expansion that all domestic savings, ploughed back into the economy, do not meet the investment expenditures required for the target growth. The very long process of narrowing the internal gap (investment–savings) may also be attributed to the rate of return on domestic investment if it is systematically lower than the cost of capital. In the case of many borrowing LDCs, various other deterrents to productivity and reinvestment may further lengthen the first stage of the debt inflow.

Considering these limitations, the author decided to expand the list of growth indices beyond only one variable, such as the internal gap (or the external gap), in this study.

INCREMENTAL CAPITAL OUTPUT RATIO

The incremental capital output ratio basically reflects the concept of efficiency on the part of the economy. This ratio reflects output growth to investment. Some conceptual difficulties surround the use of this ratio that are worth mentioning. For example, there is a difference between the average capital output ratio and the incremental capital output ratio. The average ratio is the value of the total stock of capital divided by the total output (GDP), whereas the incremental ratio is the value of new investment (additional investment) divided by the value of new output (additional output). The author prefers the ICOR over the average capital output ratio because of the following: (1) The value of the ICOR reflects the contribution of the latest capital, injected into the economy, in a period under study. (2) The changes in the values of the average capital output ratio are usually slow, whereas the values of the ICOR can vary significantly.[8] Thus the ICOR can provide a better indication of the changes in the efficiency of capital over time. (3) Belonging to the theory of "incrementalism," the use of the ICOR is popular and established in the literature.

However, a problem in using the ICOR is the time lag between the date of the new capital and the time the additional output is produced. With respect to this study, a two-year time lag has been used. This arbitrary time lag has been consistently applied to the cases of all the borrowing countries in the sample.

THE CONCEPT OF NET RESOURCE TRANSFER

There are three measurable indices for the inflow of financial resources into LDCs: gross capital inflow, net capital inflow, and net resource transfer on account of capital.

Gross capital inflow consists of various forms of capital that enter the economy before amortization of loans, interest expenses, dividends, and other outflows of capital are subtracted. Net capital inflow is derived by subtracting the amortization of foreign loans, outflow of foreign equity, and capital export form gross capital inflow. Finally, the net resource transfer on account of capital is the residual of net capital inflow minus the cost of imported capital (interest of foreign loans and dividends repatriated on foreign equity).[9]

It is the net resource transfer, rather than the gross or net capital inflow, which actually supplements the domestic resources (domestic savings) for domestic investment. Based on the same concept for foreign loans, the net resource transfer on account of debt is calculated in this study to measure the monetary contribution of foreign loans to the economy. This value, which is the residual of the disbursed loans minus amortization of the principal and interest expenses, measures the portion of the disbursed loans that remains in the economy to supplement domestic and other foreign sources.

THE GROWTH RATE OF EXPORT
AND THE RATIO OF EXPORTS TO THE GDP

There is no explicit discussion in the literature that the values of the above derived variables will change in parallel with the inflow of foreign capital or foreign loans. However, the inclusion of these variables in the list of growth indicators is not conceptually irrelevant. In the process of a self-sustained growth, export revenue will gradually replace the inflow of foreign capital. Thus the external gap (or the internal gap) will tend to narrow over time. Without the expansion of export revenue, which is a major source of foreign currency, a borrowing country will be infinitely dependent on foreign loans and/or other forms of foreign capital. Also, the derived variables of the growth rate of exports and the ratio of export to GDP reflect the extent to which a borrowing country has been successful in channeling its resources toward the export sector.

NOTES

1. Gerald M. Alter, "The Servicing of Foreign Capital Inflow by Underdeveloped Countries," in *Accelerating Investment in Developing Countries,* ed. A. N. Agarwala and S. P. Singh (Bombay: Oxford University, 1968), pp. 508–31.

2. H. B. Chenery and A. Strout, "Foreign Assistance and Economic Development," *American Economic Review* 56 (1966): 679–733.

3. See the article, similar to that of Chenery and Strout, by R. McKinnon, "Foreign Exchange Constraint in Economic Development and Efficient Aid Allocation," *Economic Journal* 74 (1964): 388–409.

4. H. B. Chenery and P. Eckstein, "Development Alternatives for Latin America," *Journal of Political Economics* 78 (July 1970): 966–1006, especially pp. 968–69.

5. D. Avramovic et al., *Economic Growth and External Debt* (Baltimore: Johns Hopkins University Press, 1964), p. 53.

6. Ibid., p. 54.

7. Ibid., p. 55.

8. Gerald M. Meier, "Criticism of the Capital-Output Ratio—Note," in *Leading Issues in Economic Development,* ed. Gerald M. Meier (New York: Oxford University Press, 1976), p. 258.

9. See D. Avramovic, "Latin American External Debt: A Study in Capital Inflows and Terms of Borrowing," *Journal of World Trade Law* 4, no. 2 (March–April 1970): 134–36.

Selected Bibliography

BOOKS

Adelman, Irma. *Practical Approaches to Development Planning: Korea's Second Five-Year Plan.* Baltimore: Johns
Hopkins University Press, 1969.

Aliber, Robert Z. *A Conceptual Approach to the Analysis
of External Debt of the Developing Countries.* Working
Paper no. 421. Washington, D.C.: World Bank, 1980.

Alter, Gerald M. "The Servicing of Foreign Capital Inflows
by Underdeveloped Countries." In *Accelerating Investment in Developing Countries,* ed. A. N. Agarwala and
S. P. Singh, pp. 508–31. Bombay: Oxford University,
1968.

Areskoug, Kaj. *External Public Borrowing: Its Role in
Economic Development.* New York: Praeger, 1969.

Avramovic, Dragoslav et al. *Economic Growth and External
Debt.* Baltimore: Johns Hopkins University Press, 1964.

Feder, Gershon. *Economic Growth, Foreign Loans and Debt
Servicing Capacity of Developing Countries.* Working
Paper no. 146. Washington, D.C.: World Bank, 1980.

Fitzgerald, E. V. K. *The Political Economy of Peru 1956–
1978.* Cambridge: Cambridge University Press, 1979.

—————. *The State and Economic Development: Peru
Since 1968.* Cambridge: Cambridge University Press,
1976.

Fleming, Alex. *Private Capital Flows to Developing Coun-
tries and Their Determination: Historical Perspective,
Recent Experience, and Future Prospects.* Working
Paper no. 484. Washington, D.C.: World Bank, 1981.

Frank, Charles R. et al. *Foreign Trade Regimes and
Economic Development: South Korea.* New York: Columbia University Press, 1975.

Hawkins, Robert G., Walker L. Ness, Jr., and Il Sakong.
*Improving the Access of Developing Countries to the
U.S. Capital Markets.* Bulletin no. 1975–4. New York:
New York University Press, 1975.

Hicks, Norman, and Paul Streeten. *Indicators of Development: The Search for a Basic Needs Yardstick.* Working
Paper no. 104. Washington, D.C.: World Bank, 1979.

125

Hong, Wontack. *Trade, Distortions and Employment Growth in Korea.* Seoul: Korean Development Institute, 1977.

Hong, Wontack, and Anne O. Krueger. *Trade and Development in Korea.* Seoul: Korean Development Institute, 1975.

Hope, Nicholas C. *Developments in and Prospects for the External Debt of the Developing Countries: 1970–1979 and Beyond.* Working Paper no. 488. Washington, D.C.: World Bank, 1981.

Jones, Leroy P., and Il Sakong. *Government, Business and Entrepreneurship in Economic Development: The Case of Korea.* Cambridge, Mass.: Harvard University Press, 1980.

Katz, Jeffrey A. *Capital Flows and Developing Country Debt.* Working Paper no. 352. Washington, D.C.: World Bank, 1979.

Kim, Seung Hee. *Foreign Capital for Economic Development.* New York: Praeger, 1970.

King, Benjamin B. *Notes on the Mechanics of Growth and Debt.* Baltimore: Johns Hopkins University Press, 1968.

Kitty, Daniel R. *Planning for Development in Peru.* New York: Praeger, 1967.

Krueger, Anne O. *The Development Role of the Foreign Sector and Aid.* Cambridge, Mass.: Harvard University Press, 1979.

Kuczynski, Pedro-Pablo. *Peruvian Democracy Under Economic Stress.* Princeton, N.J.: Princeton University Press, 1977.

Looney, Robert E. *The Economic Development of Panama.* New York: Praeger, 1976.

Mason, Edward S. et al. *The Economic and Social Modernization of the Republic of Korea.* Cambridge, Mass.: Harvard University Press, 1980.

Meier, Gerald M. "Criticism of the Capital-Output Ratio." In *Leading Issues in Economic Development,* ed. Gerald M. Meier, pp. 258–61. New York: Oxford University Press, 1976.

"Mobilizing Foreign Resources." In *Leading Issues in Economic Development,* ed. Gerald M. Meier, chap. VI, pp. 331–416. New York: Oxford University Press, 1976.

O'Brian, Richard. *Private Bank Lending to Developing Countries.* Working Paper no. 482. Washington, D.C.: World Bank, 1981.

Pagano, Carlos. *External Financing Prospects of Latin America's Development Banking System.* Washington, D.C.: Inter-American Development Bank, 1979.

Park, Yoon S. *The Euro-bond Market Function and Structure.* New York: Praeger, 1974.

Thorp, Rosemary, and Geoffrey Bertram. *Peru 1890–1977, Growth and Policy in an Open Economy.* New York: Columbia University Press, 1978.

Wade, Larry L., and B. S. Kim. *Economic Development of South Korea: The Political Economy of Success.* New York: Praeger, 1978.

Wellons, P. A. *Borrowing by Developing Countries on the Euro-currency Market.* Paris: Organization for Economic Cooperation and Development, 1977.

Westphal, Larry E., and Yong W. Rhee. *Korean Industrial Competence: Where It Came From.* Working Paper no. 469. Washington, D.C.: World Bank, 1981.

Winer, B. J. *Statistical Principles in Experimental Design.* New York: McGraw-Hill, 1971.

DISSERTATIONS

Bingardi, Faris Thabit. "External Indebtedness of the Less Developed Countries." Ph.D. dissertation, University of California, Riverside, 1977.

Blam, Yoram. "Foreign Capital Inflows, the Balance of Payments, and Economic Development." Ph.D. dissertation, New York University, 1973.

Manolescu, Friedhilde M. "External Debt and Economic Development in Brazil (1968–76)." Ph.D. dissertation, Cornell University, 1978.

Moura, Alkimar R. "Private External Borrowing: The Brazilian Experience." Ph.D. dissertation, Stanford University, 1978.

Seiber, Marilyn. "The External Debt of Developing Countries." Ph.D. dissertation, American University, 1979.

Taher, Mahmoud A. "External Borrowing and Economic Growth in Jordan During the Period 1955–75." Ph.D. dissertation, University of Illinois, Urbana-Champaign, 1979.

GOVERNMENT AND INTERNATIONAL ORGANIZATION DOCUMENTS

Asian Development Bank. *Key Indicators of Developing Member Countries of ADB 9.* April 1978.

International Bank for Reconstruction and Development. *The Current Economic Position and Prospects of Peru.* Washington, D.C., 1973.

International Monetary Fund. *International Financial Statistics Yearbook.* Washington, D.C., 1981.

―――――. *Balance of Payment Yearbook.* Washington, D.C., 1980.

―――――. *External Debt Management Policies.* Paper no. SM/79/125. Washington, D.C., 1979.

―――――. "World Bank External Debt Reporting to Cover Private, Non-Guaranteed Loans." *IMF Survey 7,* June 5, 1978, pp. 10–15.

―――――. *Peru—Recent Economic Development.* Washington, D.C., 1977.

Korea, Republic of. *Summary of the Fourth Five-Year Economic Development Plan (1977–1981).* Seoul, 1976.

―――――. *Summary of the First Five-Year Economic Development Plan (1962–1966).* Seoul.

―――――. *Summary of the Third Five-Year Economic Development Plan (1972–1976).* Seoul, 1971.

National Planning Institute. *Plan de Peru, 1975–1978.* Lima, 1975.

―――――. *Plan de Peru, 1971–1975.* Lima, 1971.

Organization for Economic Cooperation and Development. *External Indebtedness of Developing Countries: Present Situation and Future Prospects.* Paris, 1979.

Organization of American States. Inter-American Economic and Social Council. *Final Act of the CIAP Committee in Peru.* Washington, D.C., 1964.

UNCTAD. *The Concept of the Present Aid and Flow Targets.* TD/B/493/Rev. 1. 1975.

―――――. *Debt Problems in the Context of Development.* TD/B/C.3/109/Rev. 1. 1974.

World Bank. *Peru, Major Development Policy Issues and Recommendations.* Washington, D.C., 1981.

―――――. *Chile, An Economy in Transition.* Washington, D.C., 1980.

―――――. *Portugal, Current and Prospective Economic Trends.* Washington, D.C., 1978.

―――――. *Borrowing in International Capital Markets.* Various issues. Washington, D.C.

―――――. *World Debt Tables.* Various issues. Washington, D.C.

JOURNAL ARTICLES

Avramovic, Dragoslav. "Latin American External Debt: A Study in Capital Inflow and Terms of Borrowing." *Journal of World Trade Law* (March–April 1970): 134–36.

Chenery, H. B., and P. Eckstein. "Development Alternatives for Latin America." *Journal of Political Economics* (July 1970): 966–1006.

Chenery, H. B., and A. M. Strout. "Foreign Assistance and Economic Development: Reply." *American Economic Review* 58 (1968): 912–16.

————. "Foreign Assistance and Economic Development." *American Economic Review* (September 1966): 679–733.

"Financing Developing Countries' Soaring Deficits." *International Currency Review* 7 (September–October 1975): 11–14.

Giddy, Ian H., and Russ Ray. "The Eurodollar Market and the Third World." *University of Michigan Business Review* 28 (March 1976): 11–15.

Griffin, D. B. "Foreign Capital, Domestic Savings, and Economic Development." *Bulletin of the Oxford University Institute of Economics and Statistics* 32 (1970): 99–112.

Simonis, Udo E. "Some Considerations on the External Public Debt of LDCs." *Intereconomics* 7/8 (Summer 1977): 204–7.

Singer, Hans. "The Distribution of Gains Between Investing and Borrowing Countries." *AER Papers and Proceedings* 40, no. 2 (May 1970): 89–93.

Westphal, Larry E. "The Private Sector as a Principal Engine of Development: Korea." *Economic Development and the Private Sector* (September 1981): 31–35.

PERIODICALS AND MAGAZINES

"After Rescheduling, a New Solvency: Even the Anchovies Are Returning to Peru." *Euromoney* (April 1980): xi–xvi.

"Arab Banking." *Middle East Economic Digest Special Report* (August 1981).

"Financing the LDCs: The Role of the Euromarket." *Euromoney* (November 1977):76–83.

"The New Wave in Arab Banking." *Middle East Economic Digest Special Report* (November 1981).

"Peru—A Survey, Special Report." *Euromoney* (June 1980): 1–37.

"Peru: Back to Crisis." *The Economist* (March 1978): 77–78.

"Peru's Crisis, One Mistake After Another." *Euromoney* (June 1978): 95–96.

"The Role Foreign Capital Plays in Developing Asian Nations." *Asian Wall Street Journal,* June 20, 1978, p. 5.

White, J. "External Project Finance in Developing Countries: Institutional Implications of Recent Trends." *World Development* (1976).

"Why the Banks Bailed Out Peru." *Business Week,* March 21, 1977, pp. 117–18.

Index

About the Author

Ehsan Nikbakht is Assistant Professor of Finance at Hofstra University on Long Island, New York. He holds a doctoral degree (D.B.A.) from the George Washington University in Washington, D.C., and an M.B.A. from the Iran Management Center in collaboration with Harvard Business School. He taught as Assistant Professor of Financial Management at the Graduate School of Hood College in Maryland from 1979 to 1982.

Before coming to academia, Dr. Nikbakht was a senior analyst of overseas purchases and contracts at the National Iranian Oil Company in Tehran, Iran. He is currently active in research in international finance and options.